THE
TRAGIC
SINKING

—— OF ——

GLOUCESTER'S
PATRIOT

THE
TRAGIC
SINKING
— OF —
GLOUCESTER'S
PATRIOT

CAPTAIN W. RUSSELL WEBSTER, USCG (RET.)

THE
History
PRESS

Published by The History Press
Charleston, SC
www.historypress.com

Front cover: *Patriot*, formerly the *Dannielle Marie*. *Back cover, bottom*: Salvatore Eric Russo, Sal Russo's son, and Salvatore Moses Russo, a son of Matteo and Josie Russo, flanked by Orlando and Russo family members; *inset*: Gloucester's Fishermen's Memorial.

First published 2022

Manufactured in the United States

ISBN 9781467150866

Library of Congress Control Number: 2022931449

For Theresa

PREFACE

This book investigates the 2009 sinking of *Patriot*, a fishing boat out of Gloucester, Massachusetts, in which Captain Matteo Russo and his crewman and father-in-law, John Orlando, perished under mysterious circumstances. The book also explores *normalcy bias*—a psychological state that can lead rescuers to downplay a known or perceived threat and mire them in "analysis paralysis": where a watch stander over-deliberates and ends up doing nothing or delaying a response when every moment counts.

For Russo and Orlando, the fatal outcome was already decided—in every imagined scenario, they perished before the Coast Guard had been initially alerted to potential danger, so their deaths were not the direct result of normalcy bias. Still, normalcy bias indirectly factored into the case, affecting fishermen and would-be rescuers alike.

Here's what happened: Matteo Russo's wife, Josie, who co-owned the *Patriot*, alerted the Coast Guard that Matteo wasn't responsive to her mobile calls. She also reported that a fire alarm signal emanating from the boat had sounded. She knew her husband well and, as she too was from a fishing family, knew something was amiss. She was clear: things were not what they should be on that boat. Coast Guard rescue watch standers discussed for two hours and twenty-three minutes how to proceed once notified that the *Patriot* was in trouble. Without knowing that the crew was already dead, why did my former service deny and over-deliberate information that clearly showed a well-defined last known position, a searchable area and a harsh, unforgiving environment where minutes mattered? All within fifteen miles of Station

Gloucester? This meant that critical information such as the boat's last known position became obsolete in some rescuer's minds.

Regrettably, two silos of normalcy bias were at play the night the *Patriot* sank. Professional responders had denied a case existed and over-deliberated and waited for more than two hours to send planes, boats and cutters to the vicinity of where the *Patriot* had been tracked by a government fisheries law enforcement system—close to a nearby rescue station. The boat's captain took prescription drugs that might have altered his abilities, and he and his crewmember followed old risk equations by getting underway after dark and being short one crewman. It is important to note that normalcy bias resides in all humans in varying degrees and in different ways. Men customarily deny their inability to handle a situation more often than women, and women traditionally call for help earlier. In truth, members of the fishing fleet are vulnerable to normalcy bias. I've seen cases unrelated to the *Patriot* tragedy where boat captains, numbed by repeatedly accepting risk in a dangerous industry, waited too long to radio the Coast Guard for help.

Still, questions remain, with few clues for resolution. There were no traditional distress signals from a sinking vessel, no initial satellite alerts, no VHF-FM Digital Select Calling boat-to-boat-to-shore relayed distress calls, no flares and no radio transmissions, despite a well-equipped *Patriot* and more than forty years' experience between the two lost mariners. There was a much later satellite Emergency Position-Indicating Radio Beacon (EPIRB) alert from the vessel. The EPIRB likely had been hung up on the sinking vessel for some time before coming free and surfacing. Or its batteries were too weak to have its signal reach the orbiting satellites.

My deep passion for investigating episodes in contemporary Coast Guard history where normalcy bias has led to unnecessary deaths or delayed rescues stems from my background in two areas. The first is my time as a former rescue field commander with experience in more than ten thousand cases both ashore and afloat. Second is my experience as a contributor to investigations in areas of watch standers' fatigue, post-trauma stress and evaluating search and rescue boat crew risk.

I retired in January 2021, following a forty-five-year career across three federal agencies—twenty-six years in the Coast Guard and the rest with the Transportation Security Administration (TSA) and the Federal Emergency Management Agency (FEMA). My post-federal schedule allowed for the space and time to finally and thoroughly untangle the mysteries of normalcy bias as they relate to Coast Guard rescues. The sinking of the *Patriot* had long been on my radar.

As I reflect on my tenure at FEMA and the Coast Guard, I was able to draw parallels between different parties' experiences as a result of normalcy bias: delays experienced by potential disaster victims and survivors, and on the other hand, the delays and thought processes experienced by rescue watch standers.

FEMA data confirmed that age and experience do not make people less vulnerable to normalcy bias. Older Americans tend to evaluate new threats during impending storms through the lens of their past capabilities and brushes with disaster. Why else would the lion's share of victims after the 2011 Hurricane Irene be senior citizens who drowned? They erroneously explained away their risk based on past capabilities and circumstances rather than listening to public safety officials.

During my Coast Guard career, I spent more than nine and a half years undergoing U.S. Navy and Canadian Gunnery, Anti-Submarine Warfare, Tactical Action Officer and Electronic Warfare training and participating in Department of Defense (DOD) exercises during the ascent of wartime programs within the Coast Guard. This training and operational experience on two high-endurance Coast Guard cutters with wartime capabilities, as well as the Atlantic Area staff, helped me frame the analysis of underwater sounds from the *Patriot* sinking that were picked up by hydrophones designed to track critically endangered northern right whales near the Stellwagen Bank National Sanctuary.

The acoustical analysis was critical to the Coast Guard's marine casualty report and enabled the guard to exclude a scenario where a tug and tow had rammed or "overtopped" the much smaller fishing vessel *Patriot*. Overtopping is when a vessel crosses between a tug and its tow and is overturned by the tug's heavy towing hawser. My time with the U.S. Navy enabled me to interpret the *Patriot*'s engine noises to re-create the boat and its crew's final hours, minutes and seconds before the vessel hit the bottom.

This is my third book about Coast Guard watch standers and normalcy bias. In 2014, I wrote about the fishing vessel *Sol e Mar*'s sinking off the coast of Martha's Vineyard in 1990. The circumstances proved a case study in normalcy bias. The Coast Guard failed to respond to a radio call for help, linking the real call with the hoax transmission. But a senior watch stander didn't go far enough to investigate whether the garbled Mayday was an actual hoax or the real thing. There was enough information to know immediately that the two calls were transmitted from two different locations and received by different Coast Guard units, but the easy solution of denying the real case was accepted, initially.

In 2018, I wrote about the sailing vessel *Morning Dew* allision—when a moving object collides with a stationary structure—in Charleston Harbor in 1997 in which a father, his two sons and a nephew died. It was another instance of normalcy bias: their Mayday went unanswered because the initial call was explained away as a nuisance call, a radio check. Later, survivors' cries for help from the Charleston channel area were imagined to have come from a beach party in late December. And the senior decision maker also denied the very possibility that the survivors' shouts could be heard from a passing ship. During a 2019 presentation of the new book's findings, the present-day Charleston senior civilian search and rescue controller, when presented with the theory of normalcy bias as the *why* behind complacency, noted, "Yeah, it's another word for complacency." I challenge that it is not. Knowing about the phenomenon and understanding your own risk profile, whether mariner or rescuer, can positively affect the outcome of future cases and save lives.

Shortly after the January 2009 *Patriot* tragedy, I was invited to participate in a "hot wash," or after-action review, at Sector Boston. Station Gloucester, which would have been responsible for a rescue mission of the *Patriot*, fell under Sector Boston's jurisdiction. Secondly, at that time I happened to be researching the parallel mistakes from the 1990 *Sol e Mar* tragedy and the 1997 *Morning Dew* disaster, so the *Patriot* case drew me in.

At the hot wash, a 1998 report from the *Morning Dew* titled "Top Ten Search and Rescue Lessons Learned" was discussed. A colleague and friend who was involved in the case had coauthored the document, so I paid special attention to it. It was my sense that others at the hot wash were aware of the report. Some senior decision makers, however, were touting the rescue lessons as novel and ripe for adoption. It was as if they could not believe conditions of the *Morning Dew* case could happen again.

Perhaps they were reading it over as they thought about the *Patriot* case. I left that hot wash session wondering what other lessons had been lost to time. When I evaluated the lessons learned from the *Patriot* investigative materials that I had gathered from Coast Guard and public sources, including precious audio tapes, I knew I had to write about this case.

It is my hope that every Coast Guard watch stander, whether in the Coast Guard or civilian, officer or enlisted, and every mariner might read this book to understand and recognize normalcy bias and insist on changes to existing frameworks that allow these tragedies to occur time and time again. That said, any and all errors in this book are mine alone.

INTRODUCTION

This work attempts to answer two questions: Why did the *Patriot* sink? And why did the Coast Guard hesitate to send response assets after being notified that the *Patriot* was in trouble, even though it was later revealed that Russo and Orlando had perished before the Coast Guard was notified that the boat might be in trouble? The second question takes a reader through phases of *normalcy bias* as the phenomenon relates to Coast Guard rescues.

In granular detail, internal processes used in Coast Guard search and rescue missions are revealed to a civilian audience in three sections. Part I introduces the reader to Matteo Russo and John Orlando and follows events on the day of their death. Part II focuses on the Coast Guard's investigations and explores what others think may have happened that led to their deaths. In Part III, a reader will learn of tensions between the Gloucester fishing community and elements of the maritime industry. Separate chapters on Coast Guard search and rescue operations and the perspectives of several retired flag officers about the *Patriot* case—their analyses are profound—round out the book.

Those retired flag officers—a trio of admirals—contributed to the larger context that the case occupied in 2009, a vital inflection point. That's when the Coast Guard was managing multiple problems with the experience and capability of service members who were being assigned to operational units, including Sector Boston. Several preventable line-of-duty deaths of guardsmen were the catalyst for the twenty-fourth commandant, Admiral Bob Papp, the same individual who sponsored the *Patriot* administrative search and rescue investigation, to institute a new Steady the Service platform focusing on proficiency. He comments on his experience with the *Patriot* in this broader service-wide perspective. This section also provides a perspective of the law that protects the Coast Guard from being routinely sued.

Americans expect the Coast Guard to know and understand the dangerous seascapes they protect and to have the experience necessary to dynamically assess both the presence and absence of clues and make life-and-death decisions on their behalf. This book represents a continuing drive to document lessons learned for search and rescue watch standers, understanding that the greatest honor given to sailors who have lost their lives is to never forget the mistakes that have been made.

Nothing is more wrenching to a search and rescue commander—an experience I know firsthand—than knowing something could have saved a mariner in distress who later perished, either because of normalcy bias in the Coast Guard or from the mariner who delayed raising a Mayday. People need to have faith that the Coast Guard will do everything in its power to act quickly to save mariners in distress and be true to their motto: *Semper Paratus* (Always Ready). On an average day, the Coast Guard conducts forty-five rescue cases, saves ten lives and preserves $1.2 million of property. Please know that I have a deep respect for my beloved service—out of thousands of rescue missions that go well, once in a great while, normalcy bias takes over.

It is my belief that the existing decision-making matrix the Coast Guard uses is flawed, and often invites normalcy bias into a decision framework. Unlike a 911 dispatcher who is immediately able to dispense resources in an emergency, the current search and rescue system trains watch standers to await confirmation of distress from mariners they might have to rescue. But these mariners might not have the wherewithal or time to cooperate with the system and press a button, talk, launch flares or deploy a satellite beacon in an unforgiving environment, creating a delay in help at a time when seconds count. To compound the problem, that need for certainty is often exacerbated by a lack of experience, licensing and training by fishermen and other distressed parties that has been well documented by the Coast Guard in multiple investigations. It is an oft-used recipe for disaster that plays out again and again. One more element to consider: more senior watch standers were on "authorized sleep" during the critical early moments of the case, when quick decisions were essential. When awakened in the *Patriot* case, those senior decision makers rapidly launched rescue resources, for example.

Contributing to the tragedy was the satellite tracking Vessel Monitoring System (VMS), derisively referred to by fishermen as a "government ankle bracelet." It's designed to ensure fishing vessels operate in authorized fishing zones. VMS data provided rescuers a "datum" or last known position of the *Patriot*, but why wasn't a search ordered sooner? Or why didn't the local station respond of its own accord?

I had firsthand knowledge that this same VMS law enforcement system had been successfully used in a rescue case eight years prior to the 2001 sinking—when a Russian tanker ran down a fishing vessel off the coast of Maine when I was the First Coast Guard District's chief of operations. Two other Gloucester fishermen were lost at sea in that incident. In that case, the VMS law enforcement system had been used effectively to complement traditional alerting systems. The question the *Patriot* raised was why wasn't the VMS tracking system used as a primary source for decision-making for the 2009 rescue case when traditional system alerts were absent? And why weren't decades-old emergency agreements with cellphone providers executed to determine if, when and where signals were located or ceased?

This book answers many of these questions and provides insights and recommendations for future rescue watch standers and mariners alike in order to enhance chances of survival, knowing minutes matter in an inherently dangerous operating environment.

Part I

TRAGEDY

"The Salt of Gloucester"
by Gloucester poet laureate John Ronan

The sea is salt because the sea is sorrow,
As ships and men, none last or alone,
Are lost and the names tolled like sorrowful mysteries
In churches in harbors on the grief-got sea:
Patriot, a night in early January, founders

In strange, quick catastrophe. Alarms sound.
Friends first, a worried brother, rush
Out to the unguarded waters in urgent search
For two good and loving, loved men,
Full of humor and hard work, fishermen
And family both, a father and son-in-law,
Orlando, Russo, on the closely-woven boat.
At home, wives pray and wait, pain
Like held breath as lapstraked love braces
The same waves, faith-focused, growing
Fear fended off with faith and hope.
Hard news breaks. Strangers and friends,
Networks of city neighbors, gather to mend
Themselves with prayer, to talk, to mourn together,
Weep and feed the sea with the salt of Gloucester,
Yet recall how wonderfully faith says late:
Giovanni Battista and Matteo, already raised
Gracefully from the grieving sea, stand at dawn
Together, hand-in-hand, already home.[1]

1

TIME-HONORED ROUTINE

About 8:00 a.m. on Friday, January 2, 2009, Christian Rodolosi, the *Patriot* engineer, climbed aboard the fifty-four-foot fishing vessel to prepare for a 6:00 p.m. launch off State Pier in Gloucester. Christian worked for Captain Matteo Russo, thirty-six, who co-owned the *Patriot* with his wife, Josie, who was several months' pregnant. Josie's father, John Orlando, fifty-nine, himself a renowned fisherman, also worked for Matt. Matt and John were more than fellow fishermen—they were family.

State Pier, located just off Main Street, was and is the homeport of Gloucester's fishing fleet. Perched at the tip of Cape Ann, the upper ledge of Massachusetts Bay, Gloucester is along the North Shore of Boston, and in this part of the Bay State, generations of families in Gloucester and neighboring Marblehead and Salem have earned a living off sea. Captain Russo's trawler was outfitted for catches of cod, pollock, sea bass and halibut, delivered fresh to local fish markets. Gloucester was reported to be a "thriving and prospering town in the Federalist period, boasting a bank with a vault carved out of solid rock, a schoolhouse with a cupola and a two-story armory." Of those who resided in town and labored on the water, "They excel in their parties, their clubs, and also in their military parades," according to a Dr. Bentley after being entertained in 1799.[2]

As it had been for hundreds of years, on that crisp morning when Christian readied the *Patriot*, the Fish Pier was a forest of masts awaiting departure. Not far away, remnants of Christmas—from lights in windows of homes and businesses to evergreen decorations hanging from streetlights—hung over

Gloucester like a prayer, honoring the faithful who appealed to a higher order to keep their loved ones safe at sea.

People knew that Matt was a family man, and the one person he adored and cherished as much as his wife, Josie, was his son Salvatore Moses. Matt would take rides in his restored fire-engine red 1970 Mach 1 Mustang, a car he promised to his oldest son. He especially loved time with family around the fire pit and made sure young Salvatore was responsible and involved in family chores, including carrying firewood for the gatherings.[3] Salvatore was born on the third Monday in April, a Massachusetts holiday, Patriots' Day. Every year, residents of Massachusetts and Maine celebrate the 1775 battles of Lexington and Concord. The special relationship between father and son would extend to Matt's primary occupation.

Matt would encourage young Sal's inquisitiveness about fishing by bringing him onboard the *Patriot* and letting him play captain. In his final Christmas card to his son, from the week before the sinking, Matt wrote, "I love you so much, at times you drive me crazy, more times you are so easy to love." Taking his fatherly duties to everyday life, Matt even showed Salvatore the "proper way to eat an Oreo." Matt would always greet Salvatore the same way after a fishing trip, "La goia mia [my joy], my jumbo jet."[4]

Matt Russo's father-in-law, John Orlando, loved his friends and family and was unafraid to show it in his own unique ways. "Battista" to his shipmates and fishing friends, "Nonno" to his grandson Salvatore Moses, he was loud and over the top in everything he did. With his full-throated Sicilian accent, John Orlando would light up a room; "He'd announce his own arrival with 'Allo every-bod-y!'" according to Matt's brother Sal. "He would be equally energetic about being offended if his greeting was not acknowledged."[5]

John Orlando was many things but always interesting. According to Sal Russo, "He was quite the character. When John would greet you, he'd say 'How are you today? Bad, sad, glad, or good?'"[6] And the ladies drew special attention with John's charismatic sense of humor. Sal recollected, "Every time he met women, he would grab their hand as if he was going to kiss their hand, but instead, he would kiss his own hand. And no matter how many times he did this, the women would laugh and he would endear them to his humor."[7]

Matt Russo wasn't a novice. He was well respected in the Gloucester fishing community. Just a week before the *Patriot* was certified to start fishing operations on June 1, 2008, Peter Prybot from the *Gloucester Daily Times* wrote an article titled, "Matt's Got Himself a Boat!" Those who knew Matt swore that his allegiance to the powerhouse New England Patriots inspired the

Matteo Russo and son Salvatore in the *Patriot* wheelhouse underway in Gloucester Harbor. *Courtesy of Sal Russo.*

boat's new name. According to friend and shipmate Rodolosi, "Matt loved his Patriots and always put on a feed for people during the tailgates."[8] Matt's brother Sal recalled that Matt "went to Jacksonville for Super Bowl XXXIX [February 6, 2005]. We were season ticket holders. A group of us (six to eight) would tailgate before the games and Matteo would bring scallops and lobster prepped for the grill. His passion was the Patriots."[9]

The *Gloucester Daily Times* article recounted that "Russo began ground fishing summers and school vacations on his family's 77-foot western rig, the stern trawler *Mary & Josephine*, at age 13."[10] Having his own boat had always been in the forefront of his thoughts for years, and Russo opined, "I'm finally there."[11]

The boat's new captain spoke wistfully about how he and his father-in-law—both from a long line of fishing families with roots in Sicily—would use the new boat. "With the *Josephine* [his previous boat], you go out, get your daily limit of cod (800 pounds) and then come in. This involves many daily trips to and from the fishing grounds and burning fuel doing so. I don't like fishing that way. With the new boat, I can get my cod limit inshore and then move elsewhere to catch other species during the same trip. Besides

Above: The *Dannielle Marie* before Matt Russo bought the vessel and renamed it the *Patriot*. *U.S. Coast Guard sources*.

Opposite: Matteo Russo (*left*) and his father-in-law, John Orlando, stand in front of a big bag of fish on the *Mary & Josephine*, the family boat. *Courtesy of Sal Russo*.

a greater range, the *Patriot* will also allow me to fish in rougher weather, especially during the winter. Boats this size are very efficient to operate,"[12] Russo explained.

Russo told Prybot that he had named his new boat the *Patriot* by simply saying, "I'm proud to be a patriot."[13] But those who knew Russo gave different stories about why the name *Patriot* was chosen, each story with its own truth about the character of its new co-owner and captain.

Russo had changed from the original plan to get underway the following morning at 2:30 a.m., opting instead for an early evening departure time. This conflicted with Christian Rodolosi's family plans, so the *Patriot* would have to get underway at 6:00 p.m. without its engineer. Gloucester fisherman Mike Leary, who knew the *Patriot* crew well, later downplayed that the *Patriot* would sail with just two of the three normal crewmen. "Not unusual for guys to fish by themselves," he explained. "The Coast Guard made a big deal

about the third crewman not being onboard that day. There are some guys that fish by themselves."[14]

Prepping a boat for offshore fishing in winter is no small task, especially when the vessel might be well offshore. It's a huge responsibility, since fishing is one of the most dangerous industries in which to work. A 2009 National Institute for Occupational Safety and Health analysis of U.S. commercial fishing fatalities for the period 2000–2008 showed eighty-five fishermen lost their lives off New England waters, an average of nine per year. Massachusetts suffered the most casualties with forty, followed by Maine. Fatalities in New England due to vessel disasters (65 percent) were more common than in the whole United States.[15]

Rodolosi adjusted the scupper plates to prevent flooding, allowing water to drain from the deck. He ensured that the *Patriot*'s stuffing box—a gland that the boat's shaft passes through to prevent water from coming into the vessel—was as airtight as the attached seal can be. With every mechanical piece under stress and constant use, the stuffing box had to be adjusted every two or three days. Christian also reinstalled one-foot-high pen boards to make sure that Matt and John departed Gloucester quickly for Stellwagen Bank. Made of wood, these cattle-like pens were designed to provide stability for the vessel and safely and securely store ice and fish, in this case cod and a mix of other species.

John Orlando (*left*) and Matteo Russo pull ground cables off the stern net reel at dock for inspection. *Courtesy of Sal Russo.*

As a final chore, Christian readied the bilge area, clearing the bilge pump area to ensure the pumps wouldn't get clogged and changed the engine's oil and fuel filters for a smooth operation. Shortly before the captain's arrival, it was time to head home.

Around 5:00 p.m., the day well into darkness, Captain Matteo Russo turned up at State Pier and was, according to Mike Leary, in a hurry. Russo parked his car at an odd angle that "blocked other fishermen from getting by."[16] Matt had earlier told Christian, "We won't be gone long because I have to get back by 10 :00 a.m. the following morning for a family event," meaning back by midmorning on January 3.[17] Matt tailored the *Patriot*'s schedule to his personal one. His father-in-law, John Orlando, joined Matt a short time later. At 6:00 p.m., the *Patriot* was underway.

Once cleared of Gloucester Harbor, the thrum of the *Patriot*'s engine ran steady at 1,400 revolutions per minute (rpm), a normal transit speed of about thirteen knots. Then John likely took control while Matt set up to fish—their usual routine on approach to the Middle Ground fishery about fifteen miles due east of home, about a two-hour journey. Since Christian wasn't aboard, Matt and John likely alternated resting while underway. Christian said it was Matt's ritual to rest on the way out to the fishing area. John "sometimes watched a DVD, or listened to the radio. Everyone knew that it was critical to relax and get as much rest as possible before they started the back breaking work of fishing."[18] John loved to cook, and he would forego rest to prep a meal. Christian remembered that "you'd see his face light up if he saw a butterfish. He could make any fish into a delicacy."[19]

Patriot engine revolutions indicated that the vessel slowed as it approached the Middle Ground fishing area based on data recorded by northern right whale buoys deployed by the National Oceanic and Atmospheric Administration (NOAA), which actively tracks this species as a conservation measure.

Sal Russo, Josie's brother-in-law and himself a fisherman, believes that crewman John Orlando was likely piloting the vessel while Matt rested. Sal believes John woke Matt up, as was their routine, with the prospect of fresh coffee.

Once above Middle Ground just after 9:00 p.m., Matt deployed the *Patriot*'s nylon nets for a three-to-four-hour tow. Matt's brother, Sal, knew the longest they would tow would be four hours. Any longer and "Matt knew that he would end up losing two hours' time just getting the fish out of the over-full nets incrementally."[20]

The local weather buoy reported that the wind was from the west-northwest at about fifteen knots. The air temperature was thirty-two degrees Fahrenheit, and the water was forty-two degrees. Wave heights were not significant and topped out at two to three feet. It was cold, but not cold enough to worry about icing. Visibility was good at between six and eight miles.

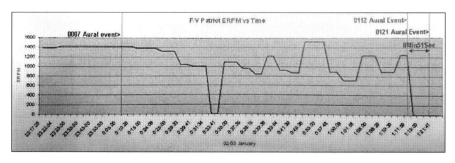

Graph of *Patriot*'s Engine Revolutions Per Minute (ERPM) from whale monitoring buoys on the night of the sinking. The ERPM graph shows that "everything was normal until it wasn't." *U.S. Coast Guard sources.*

Fishing could be monotonous given the drudgery of dragging the net, hauling in fish, sorting and cleaning them. The fish had to be carefully taken out of a large haul back to guard against bruising them. This was done using a bull rope to tie off portions of a larger haul and cinching manageable portions of the net containing fish. The fish from the cinched net would be released, culled, put in plastic orange baskets and then conveyed down into the holds. There, they were put in one hundred pound totes, and everything was covered with ice to stay fresh.

This habit of resetting the nets would start again even before the fish were put down below. Every three to four hours the routine would be repeated once they started fishing, until it was time to go back to Gloucester.

The *Patriot*'s engine surged to 3400 rpm, indicating the boat's wash down pump had been energized. Temperatures were not cold enough for direct ice formations, but Matt had apparently turned on the seawater pump to keep a load on the boat's generator and prevent hoses from freezing.

Around 10:00 p.m., Matt and Josie spoke by cellphone for about half an hour. They discussed Matt's plans to return to Gloucester the following morning around 10:00 a.m. The short trip would give Matt enough time so that they could offload the fish at the docks, finish work on the boat and be home in time for a family commitment. There was no hint of trouble on the call. Sometime around midnight, Matt and John likely saw the tug *Gulf Service* and its towed barge *Energy 11103* to their west at a range of about two and a half miles. The tug, with its 1,400-foot-long tow, was on a steady southerly course making eight knots and not going to cause the *Patriot* any trouble.

Commercial tugs had a bad reputation with most local fishermen. In 1996, the *Heather Lynn II*, a forty-five-foot fishing boat, was run over and capsized by the tug *Houma* off nearby Cape Ann. Everybody knew somebody who died on the *Heather Lynn II*. Tugs and tows were to be avoided at all cost. Matt was acutely aware of the hazards of tugs and tows, as he had salvaged and purchased the *Heather Lynn II* and fished it as the renamed *Damariscotta*. Russo told author Kate Yeomans "that he wasn't superstitious."[21] In the wee hours of January 3, about 12:30 a.m., the *Patriot*'s Vessel Monitoring System, or VMS, recorded its last location at fifteen miles east of Gloucester, right on schedule.

Rpm recordings of the *Patriot*'s engine indicated frequent speed changes. These were possibly related to a slow turn by the *Patriot*. Sal Russo believes his brother Matt might have been adjusting the boat's course and speed, reacting to the state of the tide. "If the *Patriot* is going with the tide, Matt

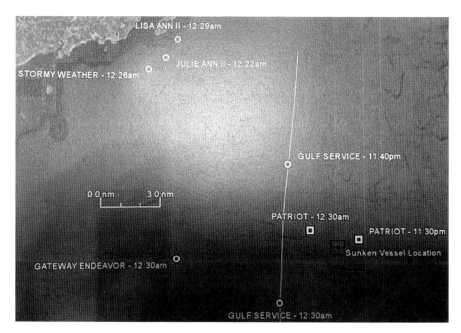

Tracks of Tug Gulf Service and *Patriot* sources the night of the sinking. The closest the two vessels came to one another was two and a half miles about 11:30 p.m., one hour and forty-five minutes before *Patriot* sank. *U.S. Coast Guard sources.*

or John would have to slow the boat down," according to Sal.[22] Sometime during the next five minutes, the *Patriot*'s power take-off was engaged, enabling power from the boat's engine to be diverted to the net-lifting winch. During these five minutes, the *Patriot*'s engine speed dropped to zero. Sal Russo assumed that "Matt or John are trying to get off a hang-up or the *Patriot*'s net has caught on a bottom obstruction like a sunken vessel. Or they have gotten their wires crossed during fishing operations."[23]

By 12:34 a.m. on January 3, the *Patriot*'s engine was at 1,100 rpm, likely indicating they were pulling in the wire beginning the end of the first cycle of fishing. Sal Russo commented that this engine speed was "kind of high" at this point, possibly causing some concern "for not overstressing and increasing the pressure in the lines." Normal engine speeds at this point of recovering the net would have been about 900–950 rpm according to Sal Russo.[24]

Between 12:35 and 12:47 a.m., Sal Russo later envisioned that the *Patriot*'s wire was being raised at this point, quickly followed by the trawl doors and then the net itself. John and Matt would be putting in the checker boards, installed on the deck and near the stern ramp after the net is retrieved to contain the catch and prevent it from going back to the ocean through the stern ramp. The cod end of the net containing the fish is then raised, and some of the fish are dumped for processing by the crew.

Recordings of the *Patriot*'s mechanical noises around 12:49 a.m. indicated an unusual spike of the boat's engine speed to 1,500 rpm and extended over an eight-minute period interspersed with "too many spikes here that may indicate the haul back is not going smoothly," according to Sal Russo. At 12:57 a.m., the *Patriot*'s engine rpm slows back into the normal range, "indicating the crew may have retrieved the net and are washing the mud off and re-engaging the power take-off motor,"[25] noted Sal Russo. By any known measure, without having to be present aboard the *Patriot*, boat operations appeared normal.

By this time, the engine noises indicated that the *Patriot* crew had recovered a full net of fish and the "net is hanging in the air," according to Russo.[26] The heavy net, engorged, is suspended, weaving and bobbing in the winter air, awaiting a careful and measured release of the catch. And then something must have happened, because by 1:12 a.m., the whale tracking buoys recording the boat's mechanical and engine noises no longer detected the *Patriot*'s engine. About thirty seconds later, something had obviously gone awry and the buoys identified a "broadband" noise that was likely the *Patriot* beginning to flood. This noise continued for approximately three minutes.[27]

At 1:17 a.m., the Wayne Alarm Company, responsible for monitoring and detecting burglaries and fires onboard boats at their docks, received a signal indicating the *Patriot* may be on fire. This alarm, likely a malfunction as a result of the boat flooding, would be the last communication of any sort from the boat until an unregistered satellite Emergency Position Indicating Radio Beacon (EPIRB) signal was received hours later. The EPIRB, designed to hydrostatically release at a certain depth, had likely gotten hung up in the *Patriot*'s rigging. The alarm company, believing the boat was at the State Pier, immediately dispatched the Gloucester Fire Department to investigate. Rodolosi, the third crewman, would not know this until later, but his uncle was one of the firemen called out to investigate the possible fire on the *Patriot*.[28]

Minutes later, NOAA acoustic buoy Number 4, the closest to the *Patriot*, detected a series of quiet events—a dull thumping—that likely signaled the *Patriot* hitting the bottom. Whatever caused the apparent sinking of the *Patriot* happened quickly and didn't allow Russo or Orlando to issue a Mayday or for them to put on cold-water immersion suits. At this moment, they were apparently alone in the cold Atlantic waters struggling for their lives. Later analysis by the Coast Guard revealed that they perished within five minutes.

Whatever happened to the *Patriot* happened quickly and was catastrophic. At about 1:30 a.m., the *Patriot* missed its hourly VMS position report. Five minutes later, Josie phoned Coast Guard Station Gloucester to report that the *Patriot*'s fire alarm had been activated. But she didn't initially inform station personnel that the Wayne Alarm Company had dispatched the Gloucester Fire Department to State Pier to check on the alarm. Josie did, however, tell the Coast Guard that Matt was aboard the *Patriot* and he was fishing with plans to return later that morning.

Minutes later, Station Gloucester attempted to contact the *Patriot* by VHF-FM radio, without success. By 1:50 a.m., Station Gloucester had requested a VMS snapshot position from Sector Boston. Assuming the *Patriot* might be at the State Pier because of the terrestrial fire alarm, Station Gloucester sent a Coast Guardsman to drive there to see if the *Patriot* was docked. The guard did not know the Gloucester Fire Department had already investigated the possibility of *Patriot* being at the State Pier at this point. By 2:10 a.m., it had been confirmed that the *Patriot* was not docked. At 2:30 a.m., Sector Boston experienced trouble accessing the VMS system but eventually requested and received the *Patriot*'s last known position from its senior command, the First Coast Guard District.

In the Coast Guard's search and rescue chain of responsibility, there is always a senior command above that can assist a watch stander. The station at Gloucester is supported and controlled by Sector Boston; the sector is supported and overseen by the District One. The Boston District accessed the system within eight minutes and determined the *Patriot* sent its last ping to law enforcement officials at 12:30 a.m. from a position fifteen miles southeast of Gloucester. By 1:30 a.m., the *Patriot* was on the bottom, and it was the only fishing vessel not checking in on the VMS.

Aboard the eighty-two-foot cutter *Flying Fish*, Boatswain's Mate Master Chief Mark Cutter, the officer in charge (OIC), was fast asleep. "It was about 2:30 a.m., and we were anchored up near Sandy Bay, Rockport, when my anchor watch boatswain's mate woke me up and told me there were several fishing boats leaving Gloucester and there was a lot of unusual 'chatter' on the VHF radio. We had no communications from Coast Guard Sector Boston on anything so I gave them a quick call and they assured me 'we're good,' so I tried to go back to sleep for 10–15 minutes."[29]

The OIC's operations officer and bunkmate, BM1 Mike Barker, recalled the unusual circumstances where their superiors at Sector Boston were giving them the brushoff—doubt and concern lingered. "Something didn't seem right," Barker noted, so "we decided we had to act."[30]

To quantify his decision, the OIC explained that the "urgency of the fishermen's communications" made the hair on the back of his neck stand up, and sleep eluded him, so he decided to act independently. The fishermen were anxiously discussing where their missing friend and shipmate, Russo, and the *Patriot* could be. "We piped 'light off the main engines and set the anchor watch' and headed to the bridge. I heard about activity in the northwest corner of Stellwagen Bank and ordered a straight-line course. We brought the boat up to full speed, 25 knots, even before the anchor was housed."[31] Something had gone terribly wrong on the *Patriot*.

I WAS INTRIGUED BY my former service's need for additional certainty in 2009, despite the forty-two-degree Atlantic Ocean water temperatures and the proximity of nearby rescue assets—much closer than in most previous cases. These water temperatures gave most mariners less than ninety minutes to live without some type of protective suit. In most rescue scenarios, without an immediate response in the *Patriot* case, Matteo Russo and John Orlando had little chance of survival.

A panicked Josie Russo called Station Gloucester again at 2:42 a.m. to report that the vessel's fire alarm system continued to alert the Wayne Alarm Company. By 3:15 a.m., Coast Guard records indicate that Station Gloucester was told by senior Sector Command to "stand down." Presumably, this was because the sector didn't think they had enough information to go on and didn't want to risk the safety of Station Gloucester personnel had they attempted a rescue. This gnashing of teeth by the Coast Guard—normalcy bias at full throttle—would later be sharply criticized. Two minutes later, Sector Boston issued an Urgent Marine Information Broadcast, essentially alerting local mariners that the *Patriot* may be in trouble and that any mariner should provide information and assistance, if possible.

In Gloucester, Dominic Orlando, Josie's brother, awakened to "panicked knocking" at his family's home at about 3:30 a.m. "My sister Grace was freaking out, standing there and talking about a fire alarm going off on the *Patriot*."[32]

2

THE SEARCH

At 3:45 a.m. on January 3, the Coast Guard's District Command recommended that "Sector Boston launch Station Gloucester because of 'close proximity.'" By 3:52 a.m., District One directed that rescue resources be launched to search the *Patriot*'s last known VMS position.

Before 4:00 a.m., Dominic had made the short trip to his sister Josie's house. Inside, Dom and Grace listened as Josie recounted catastrophic narratives that she had considered, including that the *Patriot* had sunk, an explosion had occurred or the boat had caught fire—confusion all around.[30] Shocked, the family could do nothing but wait. They just sat there, clustered, and worried. At 4:34 a.m., First District received an unregistered 121.5 MHz EPIRB signal, the only traditional distress signal thought to have originated from the *Patriot*.

Within forty-five minutes after weighing anchor, the Coast Guard Cutter *Flying Fish* arrived near where Matteo's friends in their fishing boats had clustered and a Coast Guard helicopter was just starting to close in on an EPIRB's 121.5 MHz homing signal and was in a low hover over something in the water. The Coast Guard helicopter launched around 4:40 a.m. from Air Station Cape Cod for the *Patriot* case. Bad weather had forced the delay from the first order to launch at 3:58 a.m. Every minute counts in a rescue situation.

By 5:17 a.m., a lookout from the helicopter reported seeing a lifeless body in the water in the area where the unregistered beacon emanated. The scene was naturally chaotic, and the *Flying Fish*'s OIC was surprised there were no small boat assets on scene from the nearby Coast Guard Station Gloucester.

DISTRESS SIGNALING WITH EPIRB

An Emergency Position-Indicating Radio Beacon (EPIRB) is a type of emergency locator beacon, a portable, battery-powered radio transmitter used in emergencies to locate airplanes, vessels and persons in distress and in need of immediate rescue. In the event of an emergency, such as a ship sinking or an airplane crash, the transmitter is activated and begins transmitting a continuous radio signal, which is used by search and rescue teams to quickly locate the emergency and render aid. The signal is detected by satellites operated by an international consortium of rescue services, COSPAS-SARSAT, which can detect emergency beacons anywhere on Earth transmitting on the COSPAS distress frequency of 406 MHz. The consortium calculates the position of the beacon and quickly passes the information to the appropriate local first responder organization, which performs the search and rescue. The basic purpose of this system is to help rescuers find survivors within the so-called golden day during which the majority of survivors can usually be saved. The feature distinguishing a modern EPIRB, often called GPIRB, from other types of emergency beacon is that it contains a GPS receiver and broadcasts its position, usually accurate within one hundred meters, to facilitate location. Previous emergency beacons without a GPS can only be localized to within two kilometers by the COSPAS satellites.[*]

---

[*] Bing.com, Emergency Position-Indicating Radio beacon, accessed December 13, 2021, https://www.bing.com/search?q=EPIRB&form=QBLH&sp=-1&pq=epirb&sc=9-5&qs=n&sk=&cvid=7CFDD59870BB419EB8265F85134AB7CA.

His instincts had been spot-on, and soon the chopper directed that he and his crew recover the body.

To retrieve a body at sea, the OIC had to launch *Flying Fish*'s small rigid-hull inflatable boat (RHIB) through the cutter's stern chute or notch. RHIBs on this class of Coast Guard cutter have only limited space for a two-person (coxswain and engineer) crew and very little room to work to get a lifeless body onboard. Worse, there wasn't enough space to attempt CPR, if called for, while a victim was on the RHIB.

When they found him, John Orlando was clothed but not wearing a life vest or survival suit, both of which had been aboard the *Patriot*. According to OIC, "the RHIB drove up the [*Flying Fish*'s] v-notch and the challenge became to carefully get the body [from the small boat] on to the stokes litter. Boatswain's Mate Barker (an EMT) and I performed an assessment of Mr. Orlando and talked to the on-call Flight Surgeon at the Coast Guard Air Station Cape Cod. It was our assessment based on the color and condition of the body, that we not conduct lifesaving measures. The Station Gloucester 47-foot motor lifeboat had arrived on scene about the same time the crew of the *Flying Fish* got Mr. Orlando onboard. We respectfully covered Mr. Orlando's body and continued the search for two hours looking for Captain Matt Russo."[34] After a few hours of searching, at 10:19 a.m., Sector Boston directed the OIC to bring Orlando to the nearby Station Gloucester and deliver him to the medical examiner.

Just after 6:15 a.m., Josie's family arrived at Station Gloucester to await updates. Throughout the morning, family members filtered into the station to join the vigil. Dominic later joined the family after taking his fishing boat out to search for his father, John, and brother-in-law, Matt.

John Orlando's body was transported to Station Gloucester on *Flying Fish* so the family could identify the remains and then turned over to the Boston medical examiner. Mark Cutter recalled, "When we arrived at Station Gloucester at 12:06 p.m., we were met by State Police, homicide detectives, and the M.E. The press arrived soon thereafter. Myself along with family members were brought into the Station Training Room for a Next of Kin briefing."[35]

At 12:14 p.m., a helicopter crew located Matteo Russo. Like his father-in-law, he wasn't wearing an immersion (survival) suit or life jacket. He was brought to Coast Guard Station Gloucester to be identified by family and turned over to the Boston medical examiner. At 12:48 p.m., the Coast Guard helicopter arrived at the station, and Mark Cutter and his *Flying Fish* crew assisted in removing Russo's body from the Coast Guard helicopter. "Everyone else from the station was either out on the search or consoling the families,"[36] Cutter said. At 1:02 p.m., the station would summon the local Emergency Medical Service for the grief-stricken Josie Russo.[37]

The finality of seeing the lifeless bodies of her husband, Matt, and father, John, overwhelmed Josie. She and her family members departed an hour before a 3:00 p.m. Coast Guard news briefing at the Gloucester station. Their grief and anger would accelerate as time revealed details of the Coast Guard's delayed efforts to potentially assist their loved ones. It would be several weeks before anyone would know that Matt and John could not have been saved. The Coast Guard suspended search efforts in the *Patriot* case at

John posing with a large mako shark. *Courtesy of Sal Russo*.

4:50 p.m. In later testimony, the medical examiner pinpointed the deaths of Matteo and John at about 1:22 a.m., thirteen minutes before Josie's initial call for help to Station Gloucester.

At the time of his death, John Orlando was four months from retirement. His obituary indicated that he had intended to "spend more time with family, go camping, design fishing nets, organic garden, and make wine with his son Dominic."[38]

Some people recognized John as their Sicilian historian. Christian Rodolosi remembered the time after friend and biker Dave Allen died and they all went to the funeral. Later, Dave was buried in the Italian cemetery in Gloucester. "We all walked around the cemetery—and it became John's two-hour narrative of history about everyone's family. He knew every Sicilian family. He'd say, 'There's your aunts, cousins, came over in '62.' He knew everything about everyone. Best time I ever had."[39]

John Orlando's talents didn't stop with his historical prowess or his special brand of social graces. According to longtime shipmate Sal Russo, "That man could cook. Every time we would head back from a fishing trip, he knew the guys were thinking about their wives and girlfriends and getting back together. He would cook pasta 'bombs' (with beans) to make the reunions memorable."[40]

If you asked those who knew Matt and John, they would insist that they had lived full lives, enjoying every moment with friends and family. The last voyage of the *Patriot* would leave an indelible mark on the Coast Guard—because of the lessons to be learned and memorialized in training programs and case studies for search and rescue controllers.

3

WHAT HAPPENED?

Thirteen years after the *Patriot* sinking, no definitive answer exists to explain why the boat sank. But theories abound. Why did it flood and sink? Did a submarine pull it down or a line from a tugboat rake the decks and drag it under? Did the *Patriot* become unstable? Several working hypotheses exist. Most have been explored by the Coast Guard, separate scientific entities and the Russo and Orlando families. The only way to know is if the vessel were refloated and put through forensic stability tests. Everything else is just theory and conjecture, including the government's analyses.

Here is what we know. The events of January 3, 2009, did not apparently allow Russo or Orlando time to react to the unfolding tragedy by sounding a traditional Mayday from one of their seven radios, to self-activate one of two onboard satellite distress beacons or to dial 911 (or *CG/*24) on either of their cellular phones, to shoot flares or to don immersion suits or personal flotation devices.

It's believed that the tragedy unfolded so quickly they could not climb into the *Patriot*'s life raft, which had hydrostatically sprung free from the sinking vessel. The installed life raft's hydrostatic release unit mechanism was designed to be water-activated once the *Patriot* sank to a depth of four meters. Then, when the raft moved a short distance away from the boat, the line tethering it to the vessel broke at a designed "weak link." This final jerking motion from the boat sinking triggered a carbon dioxide release that inflated the raft, and it floated to the surface.[41]

The absence of normal signs of alerting distress signals created a conundrum for the fishermen's would-be rescuers. The Coast Guard's rescue systems, for the most part, are designed by nature to require a cooperative mariner in distress to send affirmative indicators of the vessel's name, location and nature of their problems either in person or automatically by registered electronic alerting devices. Ninety percent of the mariners saved by the Coast Guard each year are rescued within twenty miles of the coastline; the *Patriot* sank within that range.

Still, in its due diligence and according to protocols, the Coast Guard released an exhaustive Marine Casualty Investigation report almost twenty months after the sinking. The report used remotely operated vehicle and government and commercial diver footage, stability modeling and a unique U.S. Navy acoustical analysis to explore the possibility of a "collision, capsize/loss of stability, or flooding" as possible causal factors to explore and explain the sinking.[42] Before and during the investigation by the Coast Guard, the Russo and Orlando families conducted their own research.

Coast Guard investigators attempted to rule out several possibilities, including a collision with another vessel. They reviewed satellite location tracking data from the *Patriot*'s Vessel Monitoring System (VMS) and tug *Gulf Service*'s commercial vessel Automatic Identification Systems (AIS). The Marine Casualty Investigation report indicated, "Because of the tug *Gulf Service*'s and barge *Energy 11103*'s close proximity to the F/V *Patriot* on January 2, 2009…investigators boarded the vessel in Piney Point, Maryland." Members of the Russo and Orlando families also homed in on the tug as a possible culprit and conducted their own plot of the vessels' movements.

Knowing the circumstances, Captain Greg Bashaw, a tugboat captain, found it odd that the families had enlisted him to help plot the *Gulf Service*'s AIS information alongside the *Patriot*'s VMS information. Bashaw had worked with John Orlando's son, Dominic, who trusted him both as a friend and as a co-worker on the tug *Merit*. According to Bashaw, "Josie and Dominic wanted answers and wanted to blame something or someone for what had happened and make sense of what had happened."[43] The tug and tow scenario made some sense early on.

Their early plot of the AIS and VMS data showed a time around 11:30 p.m. on January 2 that the two vessels came relatively close. Keeping in mind that with the 1,300-foot tow wire, the *Gulf Service* and its towed barge *Energy 11103* spanned a distance and possible threat to *Patriot* that was greater than a quarter of a mile. Couple that distance with the inherent 300-yard accuracies of AIS and VMS systems, and the initial plot made a collision somewhat of a possibility. Bashaw noted, "The tug maintains a pretty straight southerly track at about eight knots. Fishing vessels are less predictable in terms of course and speed." His plot was verified by another fishing boat captain and two family members.[44]

The government's investigation would be much more exhaustive, but the families' early efforts and the Coast Guard's announcement about the tug scenario would ignite some hope for the certainty of an understandable explanation. Coast Guard investigators at the Piney Point, Maryland location quickly scanned the *Gulf Service*'s hull from shore and the water for any signs of contact with a small fishing vessel. The report indicated, "There were no visible scrapes or gouges on the tug or barge consistent with a collision with a smaller, steel-hulled vessel."[45]

Interviews were conducted with tug crewmembers, and video from the tug's self-contained security video system was copied on DVD for the vessel's transit from Searsport, Maine, through Massachusetts Bay and on to its Maryland destination. *Gulf Service*'s camera system included three cameras mounted on the upper bridge area, with two facing aft (port and starboard views of the trailing barge) and the third camera recording directly ahead to capture the tug's movements. Analysis of the video indicated that "no other vessels were recorded by the cameras during the tug *Gulf Service*'s transit through Massachusetts Bay."[46] With the exception of a white foam lobster float with a "red flag suspended upside down" entangled on the tow cable that appeared briefly during the early morning hours of January 3, nothing was unusual on the footage. Investigators also determined that "no signs of tampering or alteration of the hard drives existed."[47]

The two-thousand-foot-long, two-inch-diameter towing cable that had connected *Gulf Service* and *Energy 11103* was seized by investigators for further analysis. A National Transportation Safety Board metallurgist analyzed the cable and determined "the condition of the tow line is consistent with typical tow operations."[48]

Joseph Abromovitz, attorney for the estate of Matt Russo and his wife, Josie, had a different opinion. Although he admitted the evidence was "circumstantial" that the *Gulf Service* sunk the *Patriot*, he indicated that underwater video from the Coast Guard left "clear indications of contact with the tow line from the barge." Abromovitz also said that the forensic examination of the cable "did not show signs of collision with the *Patriot*.... The cable disclosed nothing," but he also indicated that did not surprise him because "it was dragged through the water for 400 miles."[49]

Both the tug *Gulf Service* and its barge *Energy 11103* would undergo dry-docking eleven months after the sinking in December 2009 in Morgan

City, Louisiana, their first since prior to January 3, 2009. Investigators were present when the craft were placed in the docks. Again, the report noted, "No evidence of a collision was noted on the hull of either vessel."[50]

The Coast Guard, the Massachusetts State Police, the Orlando family and separately the Russo family would examine the damage to the *Patriot* using underwater remote operating vehicles, side scanning sonar and divers equipped with cameras. All dives on the vessel during the investigative period were approved by Sector Commander Captain Gail Kulisch, since the vessel had been placed in a Marine Safety Zone to preserve evidence and keep underwater operators safe.

The families and the media were critical of Kulisch for waiting a few days before establishing what *Gloucester Daily Times* reporter Richard Gaines characterized as a "no-go" zone around the wreck on the sandy bottom. The delay "allowed a second fishing boat to trawl by and lose its rigging to the wreck, which complicated underwater forensics."[51] Unfortunately, Sector Boston did not create the safety zone soon enough, and this led to the fishing vessel *Rhiannon Rae II* compromising the *Patriot* wreck when its fishing nets became entangled on January 4, 2009, the day after the sinking. *Rhiannon Rae II*'s Captain Fernandes, unaware that the *Patriot* had recently sunk, trawled as he usually would until 1:30 p.m. when his boat became entangled "on a large underwater obstruction."[52] *Rhiannon Rae II*'s skipper tried repeatedly to untangle his gear for over an hour, finally snapping both his port and starboard towing wires. This left his entire fishing net assembly on the *Patriot* wreck, including fishing net, ground cables and both trawl doors.

Any evidence compromised was, to the "extent of the damage this [*Rhiannon Rae II*] caused to the F/V *Patriot*…unknown," according to the Coast Guard's report. The effect of the entanglement on *Patriot* would be a continuing source of angst for the family and a subject of debate as to whether scrapes, bent materials and other impacts occurred either during a January 3 collision, upon the *Patriot* hitting the bottom or as a result of the *Rhiannon Rae II* the next day.

Despite this setback, the Coast Guard used a remotely operated vehicle, or ROV, to capture seven hours of footage of the wreck on January 30, 2009. The images included "inside the pilot house, the engine room, and underneath the starboard bow and starboard bilge keel." Family and friends of Matteo Russo and John Orlando commissioned a separate dive survey on February 10, 2009, using both video and photography. These divers also recovered the *Patriot*'s GPS unit. Over the ensuing months, the families would sponsor multiple independent additional dives to recover

Patriot at its final resting place fifteen miles east of Gloucester lying on its starboard side. *U.S. Coast Guard sources.*

items from the wreck, including a ten-ton block, the *Patriot*'s computer and the ship's wheel.[53]

In the aggregate, surveys documented the *Patriot*'s exterior and interior spaces with the exception of a five-foot-tall section of the external starboard hull due to the way the hull rested on the bottom on its right side. The report indicated that "the overall condition of the wreck appears to be good with no apparent breaches or insets on the hull." Observed damages included: paint scrapes along the port hull, including a heavy scrape on both sides of the bow; a slight bend in the top of the rudder; the pilot house showed significant scrapes and damage, including a bent radar stand and sheered antenna; and the starboard (ten-ton) block on the gallows frame has a significant bend and the wire running through it was parted.[54] There were no signs of fire or smoke inside the vessel.

The underwater surveys found that *Patriot*'s cod end of the net on the forward net reel was attached to the raised boom, indicating the accident likely occurred while a catch of fish was suspended. The cod end was not tied off to the gallows frame and was empty of fish and drifting. The forward net appeared to have jumped off its drum and entangled around the drum's axle on the port side. The wash down hose was also entangled in the net.

The *Patriot*'s outriggers were in the "up" position similar to when the vessel was in port. The report went on to note, "However, the cable spools that deploy the outriggers are 'Bird nested' indicating that the outriggers were likely down at the time of the casualty."[55]

The *Patriot*'s engine throttle was found in standby mode, and the rudder angle indicator in the pilot house was set at fifteen degrees to port. This matches the position of the rudder on the bottom. Despite what the Coast Guard report said, the families and friends could not reconcile the extent of some of the damage to the *Patriot* as anything other than damage from contact with some type of vessel. If the tug and tow theory was ruled out by the U.S. Navy underwater hydrophone and VMS and AIS tracking analyses, then who or what could the culprit be?

The Submarine Theory

Christian Rodolosi, the third crewman who missed the fateful last voyage, was flummoxed by some of the Navy's acoustical buoy data and the disfigurement of *Patriot*'s ten-ton block and a radar stand found bent in half. He looked at the acoustical data just prior to the sinking and saw that there was a ninety-second period where the engine had stalled due to being under extreme loading and could not understand it. Rodolosi wondered aloud, "Everything makes sense until it doesn't. A simple hang-up (on a bottom obstruction) by *Patriot*'s net would have only caused the engine to stall for ten to fifteen seconds."[56]

The Russo family thought the damage to the ten-ton block unusual enough to pay salvage divers to retrieve it. Sal Russo noted that "my sister-in-law Josie (Matt's widow) still has that block sitting in her garage."[57] Rodolosi and others were aware of submarines and fishing vessels occasionally interacting, often with poor outcomes for the smaller boat.

In 2001, the Japanese fisheries training vessel *Ehime Maru* was struck from underneath by the U.S. nuclear submarine *Greenville* off Hawaii, resulting in nine casualties. The submarine was performing an emergency surfacing maneuver at the time of the accident, and the *Ehime Maru* sank within five minutes. There is a history of accidental entanglements between subs and fishing boats. In 1990, four fishermen died when their trawler was dragged under by a British submarine on a training exercise off the west coast of Scotland.

A few weeks later, an American submarine ploughed into the nets of a trawler from Northern Ireland, making the vessel stop suddenly before ripping the net from its winches.[58] These accidents occurred frequently enough near Ireland that the Celtic Group made a presentation in 2020 titled, "Fishing Vessel/Submarine Interactions." The group went on to opine that it had built a "dossier of approximately 170 interactions (net snagging, towings, forced capsize and over 30 'unexplained' sinkings) since late 1980s."[59]

Such phenomena were thought to have occurred much closer to Gloucester before the *Patriot* case. On March 25, 1990, the fishing vessel *Sol e Mar* sank off Martha's Vineyard due to unexplained circumstances. Several years after the sinking, a trusted family friend indicated that a Navy official had confessed that his submarine sank the *Sol e Mar* and that he had lived with the guilt thereafter. Physical evidence also supported this report in that there was a wide debris field, and a U.S. Navy surface vessel was known to have shadowed the support vessel that hosted the families' divers who were documenting the wreck.[60] But the Coast Guard never considered this possibility in the *Patriot* case and pursued more conventional explanations at the time.

But all in all, the submarine theory in the *Patriot* case was a remote possibility given the relatively shallow 110-foot depths in the area. A submerged sub would have had minimum clearance depths from the bottom and the surface near the Middle Bank. And the Stellwagen Bank area, ripe with sensitive marine species, was an unlikely area for any U.S. Navy ship or submarine to be operating in.

The Coast Guard's Marine Safety Center (MSC) evaluated the *Patriot*'s stability and provided a report on November 20, 2009. Interviews were conducted with family members, former owners and crewmembers familiar with the boat. Complicating matters was the absence of any prior tests or marine surveys related to the boat's stability. The best the government could do would be to perform modeling to "provide some insights into the probable stability characteristics of the F/V *Patriot*."[61]

The MSC was able to create a "rough computer model of the F/V *Patriot* and assessed nine different loading scenarios for catastrophic changes to stability."[62] The end result of the MSC's effort was a finding that a combination of uneven fuel load, a raised cod end and water on the deck could have brought the vessel close to capsize. But all of this was conjecture for many people, including the grieving families who knew Matteo Russo and John Orlando had always run a tight ship with the latest safety and communications equipment. They were experienced and knew how to take care of their ship and themselves.

Flooding scenarios were also simulated by the Coast Guard MSC. The most vulnerable area for flooding was the *Patriot*'s fish hold. The report concluded, "Unrestricted flooding into the fish hold would have resulted in down flooding into the engine room and inevitable sinking." Alternatively, flooding in the engine room would have caused further water intrusion in the fish hold and inevitable sinking. Thus, MSC concluded that complete flooding of "either the fish hold or engine room would sink the vessel."[63]

Without the certainty of a submarine surfacing after the incident or a more conclusive Coast Guard Marine Casualty Investigation, the families were left with few options. Exploring legal opportunities would at minimum yield additionally discovered documents. If instability did the *Patriot* in, it wasn't the first time this would have happened to a member of the Gloucester fleet. Fifteen years before Matteo Russo and John Orlando perished, the fishing vessel *Italian Gold* sank one hundred miles east of Cape Cod on September 5, 1994. All four crewmen were lost and presumed dead. The sixty-eight-foot vessel had departed Gloucester at 8:00 p.m. on August 30, 1994, for a ten-day ground fishing trip to Georges Bank.

The *Italian Gold* was equipped with a six-person life raft, a 406-MHz satellite EPIRB, two VHF-FM radios, two long-range aids to navigation (LORAN) radio receivers, a GPS receiver, electronic chart displays and a cellular phone. The owner of the vessel, a Mr. Dimaio, contacted *Italian Gold*'s Captain Curcuru, at about 2:00 p.m. on September 4, 1994, via single side band radio. They discussed the forecasted storm that featured thirty-five-to-forty-knot winds, rain, snow and fog. They agreed the vessel would remain at sea, having previously weathered similar or heavier weather many times before. Captain Curcuru indicated the weather was fair at the time of the call and that they had "approximately 14,000 pounds of fish onboard." Mr. DiMaio indicated the vessel had been targeting monkfish along the 110-fathom curve.

Shortly after 6:00 a.m. on September 5, 1994, the *Italian Gold*'s satellite EPIRB alerted rescuers that the vessel was in trouble. A Canadian C-130 aircraft was diverted from another mission and quickly detected the EPIRB's 121.5-MHz homing beacon. The rescue plane arrived at the beacon's location at 6:52 a.m. and saw the fully capsized hull of the fishing vessel. At 8:40 a.m., Canadian rescue personnel in the C-130 aircraft witnessed the *Italian Gold* sink bow first while still overturned.

For the next four days, both Canadian and U.S. rescue forces scoured sixteen thousand square miles of ocean and retrieved the *Italian Gold*'s

EPIRB. The case was suspended after ninety-six hours, pending further developments. As with the fishing vessel *Patriot*, Coast Guard investigators explored possibilities of vessel instability as a likely culprit for the sinking, given a lack of distress calls on radio channels and the apparent sudden nature of the vessel's demise. Interviews were conducted with the owner of *Italian Gold*, the naval architect who designed the vessel, marine surveyors who had been on the boat, shipyard repair representatives from where work had been done on the vessel and previous crewmembers.

The U.S. Navy and the Coast Guard collaborated to find the *Italian Gold* using side scan sonar deployed from a buoy tender. The joint service team located the fishing vessel and conducted a video survey of the boat using an underwater remotely operated vehicle. Both the underwater ROV camera footage and eyewitness statements from the Canadian aircraft crew indicated the fishing vessel's bow and stern were fully intact but that the side shell plating in the forward area of the fish hold showed severe buckling. No bodies were seen, located or recovered from the wreck.

Similar to the *Patriot* case, the Coast Guard's Marine Safety Center in Washington, D.C., completed a damage stability analysis on the *Italian Gold*. Approximate loading conditions on the vessel were estimated using available vessel drawings. MSC's review indicated two damage conditions that would have severely affected stability. If the fish hold was damaged and flooded, the vessel would sink. Similarly, if the *Italian Gold*'s lazarette (below deck storage) was damaged and flooded, the vessel's range of stability would be greatly reduced. A stability expert who had knowledge of the area where *Italian Gold* had been fishing indicated the wave period (distance between crests of waves) was "short" due to tidal currents flowing off Georges Bank. The report indicated, "This phenomenon, coupled with winds and waves from the opposite direction, creates a steep wave pattern of high energy."[64]

While the sequence of the sinking prior to the Canadian aircraft arriving could only be reasoned, air crew testimony and ROV footage confirmed buckling on both the vessel's port and starboard sides. The report would note, "Damage was caused either by severe racking and longitudinal bending stresses experienced at the surface while attempting to ride out the storm or by the force of impact on the bottom."[65] A series of rapidly cascading events and progressive flooding was suspected.

In a final note of irony, the Coast Guard would make a safety recommendation with regard to stability to "include all Documented Commercial Fishing Industry Vessels operating beyond the boundary line." This recommendation, repeated again fifteen years later after the *Patriot* sinking, would apply to all commercial fishing vessels regardless of length.

Commercial fishing vessels that are seventy-nine feet or more in length with a keel laid after September 15, 1991, "that is substantially altered or undergoes alterations to the fishing or processing equipment must have Stability Instructions and Water/Weather tight integrity."[66] But no similar government regulations exist for smaller vessels that have alterations, nor has the government developed simplified stability evaluation methodologies. District One in Boston has, however, designed a stability course for fishermen, partnered to deliver stability training and reviewed a book with specific recommendations related to stability. The issues of stability test costs and the anticipated political and fishing community blowback continue to outweigh the current legislation written in the blood of fishermen's names etched on the Gloucester Fishermen's Memorial.

A Community Tries to Heal

Gloucester mayor Sefatia Theken pays tribute in 2021 to local fishermen who died at sea. *Author's collection.*

On August 28, 2021, a beautiful Saturday afternoon, Gloucester's Mayor Sefatia Theken presided over the annual parade to the Fishermen's Memorial. Family members of those fishermen lost at sea marched from the nearby VFW hall; many carried oars emblazoned with the names of sunken boats on the paddle ends. Each oar would be carefully placed at the base of the memorial along with flowers to honor those who perished at sea.

Speeches were given and songs were sung, all extolling the virtues and hardships of a life at sea. A young man discussed a recent loss and his own family's connection to the sea. Some attendees mourned quietly while others wept openly during the ceremony.

The mayor's remarks would reflect on her husband's continued yearning to return to the sea. She would implore the fishermen in attendance to continue to be safe and equip their vessels with the latest equipment and work cooperatively with the Coast Guard. Yet,

On August 28, 2021, at the annual Fishermen's Memorial Parade, an Honor Guard flanks oars emblazoned with names of Gloucester fishing vessels lost at sea. *Author's collection.*

2009
JOHN B. ORLANDO
JAIME ORTIZ
MATTEO A. RUSSO

2010
DUANE CHARLIE RINE

2011
PETER K. PRYBOT

Above: Sal Russo and daughter Angela next to Josephine Russo, mother of Matteo and Sal Russo, at the August 28, 2021 Fishermen's Memorial Parade. *Author's collection.*

Left: John Orlando and Matt Russo's names inscribed at the plaza near the Gloucester Fishermen's Memorial. Peter Prybot, fisherman and writer for the *Gloucester Daily Times*, also perished while fishing the same year as the *Patriot* crew. *Author's collection.*

Josie Russo and her son Salvatore Moses Russo lay a wreath at the base of the Gloucester Fishermen's Memorial as part of the 2009 Gloucester Fishermen's Memorial Parade. *Photo by Desi Smith, used with permission of the* Gloucester Daily Times.

Salvatore Eric Russo, Sal Russo's son, and Salvatore Moses Russo, a son of Matteo and Josie Russo, are flanked by Orlando and Russo family members who carry the *Patriot* oar during the 2009 Fishermen's Memorial Parade to honor the 5,300 Gloucester mariners who have died at sea. *Photo by Desi Smith, used with permission of the* Gloucester Daily Times.

Orlando and Russo family members accompany the bodies of John Orlando and Matteo Russo past the Gloucester Fishermen's memorial en route to burial ceremonies on January 8, 2009. *Photo by Kate Glass, used with permission of the* Gloucester Daily Times.

she acknowledged, the power of the sea that has no limit, regardless of safety precautions. In a final testimony to the more than 5,300 sailors from Gloucester who have lost their lives, the mayor read Isla Paschal Richardson's poem "To Those I Love":

If I should ever leave you whom I love
To go along the silent way,
Grieve not,
Nor speak of me with tears,
But laugh and talk of me as if I were beside you there.
(I'd come—I'd come, could I but find a way!
But would not tears and grief be barriers?)
And when you hear a song
Or see a bird I loved,
Please do not let the thought of me be sad
For I am loving you just as I always have
You were so good to me!
There are so many things I wanted still to do
So many things to say to you
Remember that I did not fear
It was just leaving you that was so hard to face
We cannot see beyond
But this I know;
I love you so
'twas heaven here with you!

A special banner dedicated to John Orlando and Matt Russo during the 2009 Gloucester Fishermen's Memorial Parade. *Used with the permission of GoodmorningGloucester.org.*

Part II

AFTERMATH

God performed no miracle on the New England soil. He gave the sea.

—*Samuel Eliot Morison*

4

INVESTIGATIONS

Three queries into the *Patriot* sinking were launched, each ending with compelling findings. The preliminary First Coast Guard District's Search and Rescue (SAR) case study was begun by the Sector Commander Gail Kulisch. Her report would be folded into a secondary formal search and rescue administrative investigation by the senior Coast Guard Atlantic Area Commander, Vice Admiral Robert Papp, that was concluded in June 2009. A third query, a marine casualty investigation by the Coast Guard examining likely causes of the sinking, was published in August 2010.

The investigations concluded that Orlando and Russo likely entered the water when the boat sank between 1:12 a.m. and 1:17 a.m. Josie Russo first reported to Station Gloucester that the *Patriot* might be in trouble at 1:35 a.m., some eighteen minutes later.

Even if Station Gloucester had attempted an immediate rescue attempt, there was no chance Matteo and John would have survived since the *Patriot* sank quickly, with no time to make use of the life raft or survival suits. Unlike fishermen who suffer from prolonged exposure to the elements and subsequently perish, the two men were determined to have died "within seconds" of being immersed in the forty-two-degree North Atlantic waters.

In an interview with the Boston medical examiner who performed the autopsies on Orlando and Russo, a Coast Guard investigator inquired what "seconds" meant, and the examiner responded, "Three hundred seconds," or five minutes at most. While there is no telling exactly how long the victims were in the water before they drowned, there were no signs of death by exposure or hypothermia, and neither victim had "washer woman's hands" or signs of long water immersion.[67]

Coast Guard Cold Water Exposure Models for both men indicated that they could have survived for more than an hour and a half with just a jacket in the forty-two-degree water.[68] Neither wore one, and autopsy reports revealed that both Matteo Russo and John Orlando drowned soon after the *Patriot* sank. Had Russo and Orlando worn immersion suits, they would have had a chance at survival.

Family members may have been comforted knowing their loved ones died quickly and relatively painlessly as a result of an involuntary "gasp reflex" or "cold shock" from sudden immersion that can cause rapid water ingestion into the lungs. Few people know, but death can occur within three minutes with less than half a cup of water in the lungs, according to the National Cold Water Safety Center.[69]

The Minutes

The Coast Guard concluded the timing of the sinking in a number of ways. The last law enforcement fishing Vessel Monitoring System satellite tracking signal from the *Patriot* was received at 12:30 a.m., and the boat missed its 1:30 a.m. reporting cycle, the only fishing vessel to do so.

At 1:17 a.m. on the morning of January 3, 2009, the land-based fire alarm on the fishing vessel *Patriot* activated. The alarm system was designed to send signals of possible trouble on *Patriot* over the cellular phone network. The Wayne Alarm Company was alerted, most likely when the flooding waters from the sinking vessel caused the boat's land-based fire and intrusion system to malfunction.

Weather conditions recorded from nearby surface buoys and other ships in the area indicated two-to-three-foot wave heights and fifteen-to-twenty-knot winds from the west-southwest. Air temperature was a frigid thirty-two degrees, and the water temperature was forty-two degrees. At about this same time, the Wayne Alarm Company, reacting to a 1:17 a.m. vessel alarm, unaware that the vessel was on a fishing voyage, dispatched the Gloucester Fire Department (GFD) to the *Patriot*'s home pier—but the vessel could not be located there. GFD logs of the incident reveal an engine and crew arrived at the pier area at 1:23 a.m. and searched until 1:43 a.m.[70]

The Wayne Alarm Company was notified by the fire department that the vessel could not be found. During the GFD's search for *Patriot*, the alarm company called the contact number for the vessel, reached Josie Russo and informed her of the situation. Josie Russo called Coast Guard Station Gloucester at 1:35 a.m. to report the fire alarm on the *Patriot*. She indicated the vessel was underway and was expected to return to Gloucester later this same day, January 3. The Coast Guard's investigations indicate that Mrs. Russo did not initially mention that the fire department was responding to the pier.

The Coast Guard Memorandum indicated that this initial call was fielded by a seaman at the station, who did not recognize the call as concerning a possible search and rescue case and "did not use an Initial SAR Check Sheet to obtain reporting source information." Five minutes after receiving the initial call, the seaman notified the station's officer of the day, a second-class boatswain's mate, who attempted but failed to establish contact with the *Patriot* on a VHF-FM radio. (It was later determined that this radio with a range of eleven miles probably did not have the capability of transmitting to the location where the *Patriot* sank.)[71]

The Coast Guard's Memorandum noted that while the fire alarm system had activated, no Mayday calls were received and neither of the two satellite EPIRBs on the vessel had initially transmitted a distress signal. At this point, the memorandum indicates that "Station Gloucester personnel continued to investigate, attempting to resolve the ambiguity of the situation." The station officer of the day, not yet knowing the Gloucester Fire Department had already not found the *Patriot* at its berth, dispatched two station personnel to check piers in Gloucester for the vessel; these pier-side searches continued for one and a half hours.[72]

At 1:50 a.m., Station Gloucester contacted the operations unit controller (OUCs are the senior watch standers) at Sector Boston about the situation. Sector Boston attempted to track the *Patriot* using the Vessel Monitoring System maintained by NOAA but was unable to log in and access the system. The sector then requested the VMS data from the First District. At the time the sector requested the VMS data from the Boston District, it was the first notification to the district about the *Patriot*'s situation.

According to congressional testimony, "Believing that the Station was gathering the pertinent information outlined in the Initial SAR Check Sheet," the Sector OUC also "did not use an Initial SAR Check Sheet in obtaining the information from the Station."[73] It took ten minutes for the First Coast Guard District to provide to Sector Boston the 12:30 a.m. VMS data from the *Patriot*. Sector Boston began plotting the *Patriot*'s position based on that data and, believing the case had moved from the Uncertainty to the Alert phase (in an Uncertainty-Alert-Distress progression), at 2:40 a.m., initiated radio call-outs for the *Patriot* using radio high sites that should have reached the vessel. The district controller had already asked the company that serviced the *Patriot*'s Vessel Monitoring System to email the vessel.

At the same time, Station Gloucester, Sector Boston and the Boston District all attempted to contact or locate the *Patriot*. Unaware that Station Gloucester had contact with Josie Russo—the *Patriot*'s co-owner—Sector Boston also spent fifteen minutes trying to locate the *Patriot*'s owner (even calling the former owner who had sold the vessel to the Russo family).

Discussion about the last known VMS position was now more than two hours old. Josie Russo was eventually contacted by Sector Boston OUC. She informed the sector that the burglar alarm on *Patriot* had activated the day before and that her husband's cellphone was going straight to voice mail, unusual for him.

Almost an hour and a half after Josie Russo's initial call, Sector Boston's OUC "did not believe he had a reasonable search area to allow for the launching of Search and Rescue Units," but the district controller "stated he believed they did have a reasonable search area and that Sector Boston should consider launching an aircraft from Air Station Cape Cod." However, the "Sector Boston OUC stated he wanted to make a few more phone calls prior to directing a launch."[74]

At 3:17 a.m., the sector issued an Urgent Marine Information Broadcast (UMIB). According to the Coast Guard's SAR addendum, the bible for rescue operations, "UMIBs are designed as a tool used by Coast Guard SAR Mission Coordinators [Sector Boston in this case] to alert the maritime public to a distress or potential distress situation."[75] They are mandatory in the circumstance of a vessel reported overdue.

The investigative memorandum indicated that "Sector Boston OUC still did not believe the case had moved into the Distress phase because there was no (affirmative) indication that the vessel was in distress." Between 3:30 a.m. and 3:35 a.m., the Sector and District OUCs discussed what was then known about the case—including the failure of the email (to the boat via the VMS) to elicit a response.[76]

The report also indicated that the *Patriot* was the only vessel on VMS whose position was not updating in the system. The District OUC at this point "recommended briefing the Chain of Command, and recommended launching aircraft." The Sector and District OUCs then "discussed the proper search object for the search patterns." Both the sector and district senior watch personnel would wait to discuss the case with the chain of command before launching resources even though they could have done so under their own authorities.[77]

At 3:34 a.m., the Sector Boston's OUC "woke the Command Duty Officer (CDO) and asked the CDO to come to the watch floor." At 3:43 a.m., the sector and district personnel "briefed their respective CDOs regarding the case." Between 3:50 a.m. and 3:57 a.m., a number of briefings were held throughout the chain of command at both the sector and the district levels.[78]

The memorandum indicated that when the acting command center supervisor, a civilian, at the first district, was briefed, the supervisor "recommended immediate launch of assets," which was "approximately 45 minutes after the first recommendation by the First District Command Center to launch an aircraft." A number of rescue units were launched beginning at 3:57 a.m., both air and surface assets. Good Samaritan vessels had already begun responding to the Coast Guard's Urgent Marine Information Broadcast and indicated that they were underway toward the *Patriot*'s last known position.[79]

Rick Bartlett, an experienced Coast Guard and state of Maryland rescue pilot, believed the sequence of events at Coast Guard Air Station Cape Cod went like this: early on the morning of the *Patriot*'s sinking, at 3:58 a.m., the phone rang next to the Coast Guard aircraft commander's bed in the duty crew berthing area. Awoken from a deep sleep, and a bit foggy for a few seconds, he listened intently. The Air Station duty officer is on the phone alerting him to a possible vessel in distress. By this time, District One in Boston, in charge of aviation resources that support multiple Coast Guard sectors, has cleared the launch but needs the aircrew's evaluation of the weather.[80]

The aircraft commander goes through his rote questions: How far is the vessel offshore? Is there a confirmed distress, or is it just a possible overdue vessel? Have the Air Station operations officer or commanding officer already made a call on risk assessment? In short, the aircraft commander is assessing the risk-reward equation: how much risk to self, the crew, a multimillion-dollar aircraft versus the degree of difficulty or certainty that mariners are even in distress?[81]

At 4:34 a.m., the First District received a traditional distress alert homing signal from a 121.5-MHz beacon usually associated with a satellite EPIRB. Six minutes later, a helicopter was launched from Air Station Cape Cod; launch time had been slowed to forty-two minutes from initial launch order (twelve minutes slower than the standard thirty-minute launch time) due to poor weather conditions. Launching a rescue chopper is a complicated process.

TAKING FLIGHT

Coast Guard flight crews maintain a rigorous schedule when scheduled for rescue duty. They're always aware that they are tethered to their version of a basketball shot clock. A life and death shot clock. Thirty minutes to launch and two hours to get to the search area no matter what time of day or night once the rescue claxon is activated. That standard for launch has enabled the venerable service to rescue more than one million people in distress as of 2007.

A nighttime routine has the duty aircraft commander "turning in" for the evening at 10:00 p.m. For the *Patriot* case, he might have thought the weather was likely too poor to launch for the remainder of the evening and hoped no calls for distress would test his skills this night. The common lament for aviators in Alaska and New England at this time of year is "I hope this isn't a Distinguished Flying Cross or Air Medal night," meaning an adrenalin-filled night where every reaction and every decision may mean the difference between fishermen being rescued, or in the worst scenario, the aircraft and its crew needing to be rescued as well.[82]

The work is dangerous—that goes without saying. Such was the case of a Coast Guard air crew on February 18, 1979, when their HH-3 Sikorsky helicopter crashed with five crewmen onboard while they were attempting a medical evacuation from a Japanese fishing vessel 180 miles southeast of Cape Cod. The aircraft experienced a loss of power and was forced to conduct a water landing in heavy seas and overturned, killing four of the crew.[83] Just one month after the *Patriot* sank, the lone aircraft survivor from the 1979 rescue crash, along with families and friends of the deceased, all gathered in Falmouth, Massachusetts, for a seaside memorial to remember those who had died thirty years before.

THE STAAR MODEL

One of the risk assessment models the Coast Guard developed after a series of deadly mishaps around the time of the *Patriot* case was the STAAR model (Spread out, Transfer, Avoid, Accept and Reduce) to "identify hazards and explore mitigation strategies during risk assessments."[84] Essentially, the model asks the salient question about a contemplated rescue: Is the risk worth the reward depending on what is happening at sea? Today, rescuers spread out the risk by moving units inland in advance of a storm. They transfer the risk to another agency or unit, perhaps a more capable boat when aviation thresholds are exceeded. They avoid the risk altogether by declining the mission. Rescuers accept the risk and carry out the mission, or reduce the overall risk, perhaps by waiting a few hours for daylight or better weather. In every case, a formal risk assessment score card is created and filed with each crewmember providing input in the planning stage or reevaluated at any point in the execution of the case.

The pilot responds to the initial wakeup call, "OK, I'm headed to the OPCEN. I'm going to wake the rest of the crew." The aircraft commander steps into his flight suit and boots, knocks on the doors of duty copilot, flight mechanic and rescue swimmer to make sure they're up. All four are directed to meet up at the Air Station Operations Center (OPCEN). At the OPCEN, the Air Station duty officer briefs the entire air crew on the latest details—it's an unconfirmed distress, no Mayday, but a remote vessel fire alarm has been received and no EPIRB signals have been received. We only have a three-and-a-half-hour-old satellite position from the Vessel Monitoring System fourteen miles southeast of Gloucester. Two experienced fishermen with a well-equipped boat may be in trouble just off the coast near Gloucester.[85]

The aircraft commander takes another look at all weather sources, paying particular attention to the winds, visibility, temperatures and the possibility for icing conditions. He begins to run through the 2009 Aircrew Risk Assessment checklist to make sure it's safe to fly. He considers all factors: weather, aircraft status, crew fatigue, distance to scene, availability of backup helicopter and a fixed wing "cover" flight, fuel requirements and extra gear requirements (trail line weight bags, flares, pumps, etc.).

This review results in a numerical risk score and a color-coded (green, amber, red) GO/NO GO call by the aircraft commander. If it is evaluated as red, higher approval is required by the Air Station operations officer or his commanding officer in order to launch. This particular launch is rated amber, so they are cleared to launch if the aircraft commander is comfortable.

The "ready" helicopter is towed onto the icy ramp and parked on ice chocks to prevent slippage during the aircraft's rotor engagement. The rotor wash on rescue helicopters is significant, and without restraining devices, the aircraft can move before the pilot and crew are ready. The air crew meets together at the helicopter after donning their dry suits and grabbing the duty night vision goggles. The aircraft commander then does one last poll of all his crew for their final input on risk assessment, and solicits concerns and recommendations. All four must be in agreement to proceed or the mission is put on hold until the issue is resolved.

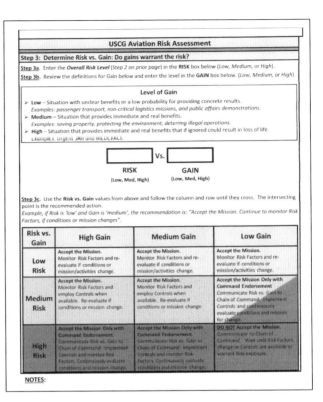

A U.S. Coast Guard Aviation Risk Assessment model typically used at the time of the *Patriot*'s 2009 sinking. *U.S. Coast Guard sources.*

The crew climbs into the helicopter and conducts the engine startup checklists, establishing radio contact with Air Station Operations Center, then a call is made to the Coast Guard Communications Station (COMMSTA) that will provide the helicopter's radio "guard" during the flight. The COMMSTA will call the helicopter every thirty minutes to ensure the crew is safe and not in trouble. A missed communications check will cause "lost communications" procedures to be declared, and if no response is received, eventually the helicopter will become the subject of a search effort. The flight is delayed twelve minutes due to weather. Once the weather improves, the helicopter and crew proceed to the scene at a low enough altitude clear of clouds to avoid icing.[86]

Almost immediately after the helicopter nears the *Patriot*'s last VMS position, an unregistered EPIRB signal is detected and homed in on at 5:08 a.m. Within nine minutes, the helicopter's crew reports seeing a lifeless person in the water. The body was recovered by the Coast Guard cutter *Flying Fish*. The deceased person, Orlando, was not wearing any type of immersion (survival) suit or life jacket.[87]

The second person on the *Patriot*, Russo, was located by the helicopter at 12:14 p.m. He was not wearing an immersion (survival) suit or life jacket. His cause of death, drowning, was identical to Orlando's cause of death. At 7:19 a.m., the fishing vessel *Cadarina G.* reports an "object 90–100 feet underwater—not fish, in position 42-24.47 North and 070-27.24 West."[88]

Why Did Watch Standers Struggle?

Even if there was no chance the Coast Guard could have saved Matteo and John, why did the Coast Guard apparently stumble badly in its efforts to understand these two seasoned mariners were in distress and urgently needed help? To what degree was normalcy bias at play? Here is what I think the Coast Guard ought to have done. They should have listened to Josie closely and recognized she was a legitimate source from a fishing family and immediately verified the last known position from the VMS to see how close the position was to Station Gloucester. They should have checked with the mobile phone company whether Russo's phone was still pinging and, if not, when and where it stopped pinging.

Those data points would have provided a composite last known position. Considering the harsh environment, all this could have been done concurrent with checking the pier (not knowing the GFD had already done so). Station Gloucester boat resources could have been on site within an hour, if not less. And had Russo and Orlando been in survival suits or the life raft, they might have been saved. And if the Coast Guard had acted with a bias for action, the service would not have had egg on its face, even if the mariners died.

Moving on, the in-depth and complex investigations focused on the timeline, existing Coast Guard rescue procedures and technologies, like puzzle pieces that needed to be assembled. Really, any element that was engaged in a potential rescue underwent a thorough vetting. We will start with technology.

New VHF-FM radios, the main lifeline for mariners in trouble within twenty miles of coastlines, were required in 2009 to have Digital Select Calling (DSC) features. DSC enables a set of pre-scripted 911-type features that allow mariners to manually activate a single red button and have the radio automatically begin continuously transmitting the vessel's name, location (if connected to a navigation system) and nature of distress to nearby vessels and the Coast Guard. These features enable a mariner to activate the rescue system within five seconds and get back to saving the boat or themselves. But Russo and Orlando apparently did not have five seconds to trigger the DSC alerting system. They likely were managing the chaos on deck, but we will never know for sure.

The equivalent of DSC on land is when a homeowner picks up their landline (not cellphone), dials 911, yells "Fire!" and then runs out of the house. The 911 calling system for permanent home numbers has the location of the problem, and the call itself can activate the first responder system.

But no such signals from *Patriot* were received until much later, at 4:43 a.m., almost three hours after the sinking, when an unregistered satellite EPIRB signal in the area of the *Patriot*'s debris field was received. Instead, Coast Guard rescue personnel were left to struggle with the absence of normal indicators. Hidden object games are popular at parties and online gaming sites. Similarly, sea rescuers are trained to pick up on affirmative clues that are very similar to the listed hidden objects in the games. Look for these particular clues and objects and click on the mouse, win the game and save the mariner, in theory.

The problem with the *Patriot* case was rescuers were looking at the mosaic of missing pieces, a situation that requires greater intuition and experience. This was not a game, and with cold water temperatures, there was little margin for error or delay. Coast Guard watch standers would have had to think critically and innovatively.

THE INVESTIGATION

Within three days of the tragedy, Captain Craig Gilbert, the chief of search and rescue at Coast Guard District One, directed Captain Kulisch at nearby Sector Boston to conduct a case study with the "sole purpose to improve the SAR system." The memorandum also indicated that the goal was to "improve performance at all levels."[89] A few days later, the First Coast Guard District released a press release quoting Sector Commander Kulisch, "In a never-ending pursuit to improve our response to mariners in distress, the Coast Guard frequently conducts this type of review to ensure protocols were observed, procedures were followed, and standards for response were met."[90]

No timeline for completion was established, and the memorandum ended with the kindly adieu, "Your attention to this matter is greatly appreciated."[91] The tone and nature of the Coast Guard's correspondence and the seriousness of the effort would rapidly escalate as the media and the *Patriot* families demanded answers. The timbre and urgency of the government's efforts were soon to take a turn with urging from the highest level of authority.

The rescue case wasn't the venerable service's finest hour. Within days, the media and the Coast Guard's twenty-third commandant, Admiral Thad Allen, called for a greater understanding about what happened and why the government's response was apparently so slow. Allen posited queries through his senior staff reacting to a January 7, 2009 *Gloucester Daily Times* article titled "Coast Guard, MSP (Massachusetts State Police) Owe a Full Probe into *Patriot* Sinking."

The commandant's nickname from his earliest days among his Coast Guard Academy friends was "Thad-miral," demonstrating that his peers knew he was always destined for additional responsibilities and more senior positions. His direct approach coupled with a strategic view would shape the organization for decades to come and would become his trademark. Best known for his extraordinary accomplishments as the national incident commander for Hurricanes Katrina and Rita and the Deepwater Horizon oil spill, the service chief wanted answers.

The commandant turned to his eventual successor, (then) Vice Admiral Robert J. Papp, for answers. Papp was the Atlantic Area commander, the boss of First District Commander, Rear Admiral Dale Gabel. Reacting the same day as the January 7, 2009 *Gloucester Daily Times* opinion piece, Allen "expressed an interest in this case this morning."[92]

The internal correspondence with subject "taskers from Commandant Coast Guard" left no ambiguity, specifically wanted to see "a timeline of the response" and asked for an information brief the next day on "our criteria for engaging in underwater investigations to obtain forensic evidence."[93] Suddenly, interest had escalated from Captain Kulisch at the sector to her boss's boss's boss's boss.

The fuse had been lit by an article that implored the Coast Guard to self-examine to determine "if different protocols could have put resources on the way in less than two and a half hours."[94] The Coast Guard would examine its performance after the *Patriot* case and would come to some honest and damning conclusions.

Vice Admiral Papp quickly exercised his authority as the senior field officer and initiated the formal administrative search and rescue investigation once he determined the level and extent to which the First Coast Guard District (northeastern area) had been involved in the *Patriot* case. Papp included the First District's search and rescue case study as an enclosure to his final action memorandum detailing his findings as part of the administrative investigation. Papp's investigation found extensive flaws in procedures and among its rescue personnel. The investigations revealed that the two fishermen had no chance of survival even if there had been no rescue miscues in a case that was challenging and complex for several reasons.

Five months after the *Patriot* sank, the Atlantic Area commander, VADM Robert Papp, published his final action on the administrative investigation of the Coast Guard's response to the sinking of the fishing vessel *Patriot*. A longer, more detailed Coast Guard Marine Casualty Investigation that explored the possible causes of the sinking would not be published for another fourteen months.

Papp's investigation was comprehensive and at times a difficult self-assessment of the Coast Guard's procedural search and rescue gaps; it detailed service watch stander human mistakes and weaknesses. In some ways, it was unprecedented. The report included several opinions and recommendations that were designed to improve the rescue system.

THE SEARCH AND RESCUE REPORT

The report found that Sector Boston watch standers missed a key opportunity to conduct a follow-up interview with the reporting source, Josie Russo, and initially deferred to a junior person with less search and rescue experience at Station Gloucester. The report indicated, "This information would have likely raised the level of concern earlier and saved valuable time processing the case."[95]

The two most senior search and rescue watch standers, the command duty officers at both the sector and District One, were seeking authorized sleep during their twenty-four-hour shifts. The report went on to say that the watch standers' inexperience "may have played a role in the relatively inefficient processing and analysis of case information."[96] In other words, the three younger, less experienced SAR professionals struggled to recognize that the *Patriot* might have been in trouble, and this ultimately delayed the launch of rescue units.

Information Overload Delays a Response

The report indicated that the key watch stander at the Boston Sector "was overwhelmed by the number of phone calls in a relatively short period of time in managing this case, and this more than likely contributed to his inability to fully process and understand the aggregate picture in the case."[97] The senior sector watch stander, the operations unit controller (OUC) managing the case, had handled more than forty phone calls between 1:50 a.m. and 5:28 a.m. The report would indicate this was "compounded by the Sector Communications watch stander and the Sector Unit Controller [the two junior watch standers] had limited experience and thus limited ability to assist the Sector OUC."[98] In truth, the one senior Sector Boston watch stander had been overwhelmed by the volume of functional calls and had little time to process or critically think about what he was being told or heard.

Should the Family Sue the Coast Guard?

It's not unheard of for bereaved families to sue when they believe the Coast Guard failed to rescue their loved ones. No lawsuit was forthcoming from the Orlando or Russo families. Still, no amount of money would bring back the two beloved fishermen. But should they sue? A court case could determine to a finer degree of certainty the cause of the sinking; provide family members closure; hold those responsible, accountable; and compensate the loved ones for their loss. But who should the families sue?

The case against the government would never be easy since laws historically favored the Coast Guard. The courts, too, generally favored the Coast Guard, understanding that a rescue agency that was routinely legally scrutinized in hindsight would be an organization severely restricted in its ability to accomplish its mission. In most cases, even a case where the Coast Guard *should* have launched a rescue sooner, the government wouldn't normally be held at fault as long as the search that was eventually launched was conducted professionally.

The precedent for the Orlando and Russo lawyers to consider legal action came from the Coast Guard's negligence when it towed the fishing vessel *Barbara and Gail* across Nantucket's Rose and Crown shoals in the early morning hours of December 19, 1961. In that case, an inexperienced Coast Guard cutter captain relied on faulty navigation readings and had not asked the more seasoned skipper from the *Barbara and Gail* for his navigation information. Five of the fishing boat's ten crew would perish in the calamity when their boat sank after having been dragged across the shoal by the Coast Guard.

In a 1966 District Court judgment, Judge Caffrey found that the Coast Guard had breached its "obligation either to send out a properly equipped vessel to assist the *Barbara and Gail* or to notify the fishing vessel's skipper that it could not assist him." Judge Caffrey added, "The Coast Guard is liable for damages caused by its negligence to any mariners who in fact have relied on the availability of its search and rescue services."[99]

Judge Caffrey's final ruling set the stage for the Orlando and Russo family lawyers to consider legal action. His decision determined that the sole cause of the sinking of the *Barbara and Gail* was the negligence of the Coast Guard. The judge ruled that the Coast Guard's officers had failed to use good judgment and had the responsibility to oversee the rescue and make solid decisions. But the circumstances surrounding the *Patriot*'s poor rescue response did not stack up well as a solid case for the families. There was, however, at least one other comparative case where family members successfully sued the Coast Guard that could guide the Orlando and Russo family lawyers.

In a landmark 1998 case, *Hurd v. United States*, the Cornett and Hurd families successfully sued the Coast Guard for $19.5 million when the *Morning Dew*, a thirty-four-foot sailboat, rammed Charleston's north jetty and a father, his two sons and a nephew perished.

Laying out the brutal reality of federal law, government lawyer Kossow argued, "The Coast Guard did not have an affirmative requirement to launch a rescue at all. Further, that the *Morning Dew* case was not about what the Coast Guard *should* have done, but what they, in fact, did do."[100]

According to Kossow, "This case, unfortunately, is nothing more than an explicit reminder to the would-be seafarer. That he should not venture blindly into unfamiliar waters armed with the simple faith that the Coast Guard will extricate him from his self-made dilemmas wherever and whenever they occur."[101] Essentially, the government was suggesting that the Coast Guard, legally, was under no obligation to render aid and assistance and mariners should not rely solely on the government if they get in trouble. And the government was placing some responsibility with the owner of the vessel.

In the *Morning Dew* case, however, the presiding judge ruled that the Coast Guard had, in fact, launched a rescue. And the venerable service had been negligent in its rescue efforts when they allowed a local pilot boat, their rescue proxy, to suspend search efforts for three of the four survivors before sunrise. The judge in the case reduced the families' original requested amount because evidence suggested that only the three juveniles in the tragedy survived the original allision with the jetty. The father, who was driving the vessel in this case, was thought to have died from impact injuries shortly after the crash; therefore, he could not have been rescued and was ineligible for monetary compensation.

Despite the harsh realities of the Coast Guard's own self-critique of its poorly timed and executed rescue efforts, suing the Coast Guard in the *Patriot* case would be a nonstarter. The grim reality of the *Patriot's* demise was that co-owner Josie notified the Coast Guard of trouble on the boat at 1:35 a.m., after the Wayne Alarm Company notified her that the boat's fire alarm was alerting trouble. The government had solid evidence from the NOAA northern right whale underwater acoustic information and the U.S. Navy's analysis that the *Patriot* had sunk between 1:12 and 1:17 a.m. The sinking likely caused the remote alarm system to fault and trigger a cellular alert shortly thereafter.

Couple this information with the medical examiners' report that indicated both John Orlando and Matt Russo died almost immediately after the boat sank, similar to the father in the 1997 *Morning Dew* case (who was thought to have died when the sailboat hit a jetty), and there was no chance for the Coast Guard to save either fisherman. Simply stated, as there was no opportunity for the Coast Guard to save Russo and Orlando, it meant that no matter how delayed the Coast Guard response might have been, there would be no legal case.

5

LESSONS LEARNED

The Coast Guard had concluded multiple informal and legal memoranda with cellular companies to help locate lost or distressed mariners since its inaugural efforts out of Hawaii as early as 1986. That's more than twenty-three years prior to the *Patriot* case. At the time, the Fourteenth Coast Guard District (Honolulu) Chief of Telecommunications had pioneered the relationships that first enabled cellular companies to use government property to situate cell towers in exchange for free service and cellphone equipment for the government's official business. Part of these agreements included the very first arrangements where technicians could be dispatched to cellular towers to obtain critical use and location forensic data for distressed mariners.

More than two decades later, and with refined and simplified remote access and legal procedures in place, the sector and Boston District watch standers were "so preoccupied with using the VMS [Vessel Monitoring System] to ascertain [the *Patriot*'s] last known position, they failed to simultaneously explore if the cellular service provider of Mr. Russo's cellular phone could have given rescuers information that would have assisted them in developing a reasonable search area."[102] Depending on the quality of the cellular information, rescuers might have seen that Matt Russo's phone stopped pinging somewhere geographically close to the *Patriot*'s last 12:30 a.m. VMS location or determined the vessel had pulled into another port.

There were at least three instances where the district watch stander, senior to the sector watch stander, made recommendations to launch rescue units and consistently deferred to the sector rather than wresting SAR mission coordinator (SMC) responsibilities. According to the Coast Guard Addendum, the SAR bible, "the SMC within the Coast Guard operates within the SAR chain of command as the person assigned to carry out all aspects of planning, coordinating and managing the response to a SAR incident."[103] The district being senior to the sector could have and should have taken SMC for the *Patriot* case and launched rescue units earlier.

In light of all this information, VADM Papp ordered the following actions to "prevent recurrence and optimize Atlantic Area SAR response in future cases, and to make recommendations for potential Coast Guard–wide improvements."[104] The admiral's report required that an instruction be developed governing VMS training usage at districts and sectors within the Atlantic Area. The report recommended that the Atlantic Area instruction include the creation of a "personnel qualification system (PQS)" and be forwarded to Coast Guard Headquarters for possible national adoption. The report went on to require that at least one watch stander on every watch have the ability to access VMS during the watch and be proficient in its use.

Soon after, Richard Gaines from the *Gloucester Daily Times* quoted the admiral, who said, "At the time of the incident, 'knowledge of VMS' or demonstration of proficiency in its use was not required by any (Coast Guard standard). The only performance standard requirement was for the commanding officer and the situation unit controller to have access to VMS." The admiral went on to note, "But, they [watch standers] were not required to demonstrate any proficiency in its use or knowledge of its capabilities and limitations. Such ignorance, the admiral indicated, should not be perpetuated under the policies on VMS written as a legacy to the *Patriot*'s loss."[105]

THE TWENTY-FOUR-HOUR WATCH: AN OLD 1999 LESSON

When senior search and rescue people were awakened from authorized sleep at the district and sector during the *Patriot* case, decisions were immediately made. Vice Admiral Papp mandated that all five of his districts perform an assessment to determine if any watch standers were operating in twenty-four-hour watch rotations or if "any Command Center position and whether Command Center Duty Officers (CDOs) were SAR qualified."[106]

Once the baseline was determined, "every effort shall be made to convert 24-hour watch positions to 12-hour watch positions." Unfortunately, the Coast Guard was relearning an old lesson.

Prior to 2006, Coast Guard sectors were formed to join two types of command units in order to optimize multi-mission performance. This blending of units and staff types and numbers was also thought to address, in part, a 1999 fatigue analysis that determined twenty-four-hour senior personnel at groups (the sectors' predecessor organizations handling SAR) were sometimes in either their "Red Zones" for performance and decision-making or alternatively seeking authorized rest at critical times during rescue cases. The study concluded that "prolonged performance in the Red Zone will lead to human error and can significantly reduce the safety of personnel and the maritime community."[107] The *Patriot* case exemplified that the manpower problem had not been fully resolved.

EXPERIENCE MATTERS

Why were more senior personnel who later became involved in the SAR decision-making process able to immediately suspect that the *Patriot* was in distress and urgently needed help? Why had the less experienced watch standers not acted on their own authorities and ruminated for hours when Russo and Orlando were within thirty minutes of the Gloucester rescue station? Why had the junior watch standers hesitated to wake up their more seasoned supervisors?

The SAR experience for the three *Patriot* watch standers who worked the case until senior personnel were wakened was less than two and a half years, total. Admiral Papp asked that a memorandum to headquarters be prepared to detail "concerns raised by this incident and the need to review the need for dedicated CDO billets at District and Sector Command Centers."[108]

Articulating the difference between well-intentioned novices armed with check sheets and quick response cards and seasoned SAR veterans, the Atlantic Area commander opined that these check sheets "cannot provide the confidence to act in the face of uncertainty."[109] The admiral's memorandum suggested that a work group be formed to "rapidly address the issue of inexperienced Command Center personnel and request the development of methods to counteract this trend."[110]

Admiral Papp's memorandum ended by sending a copy of his investigation to the National Search and Rescue School to "share lessons learned and best practices to benefit the SAR System. My goal is to foster continuous improvement, which is the hallmark of Coast Guard Search and Rescue."[111]

In the report's final paragraphs, the Atlantic Area commander directed those members at the "District, Sector and Station who participated in the response to the *Patriot* case shall personally review the findings, opinions and actions directed in this memorandum."[112] Papp also energized his subordinate field admirals by requiring each of them to personally review the findings with their command center personnel and command cadre, in essence, a safety stand-down.

Cutting to the chase of the Coast Guard's failures in the *Patriot* case, VADM Papp intoned, "We as Coast Guardsmen should lean forward with that same sense of urgency and decisiveness, guided by our principles of on scene initiative and managed risk, understanding that in every search and rescue case, time is of the essence."[113]

A Different Opinion

Captain Craig Gilbert (Retired), Captain Kulisch's immediate superior, was the District One chief of search and rescue and viewed VADM Papp's report from a different perspective. His earliest thoughts on the morning of January 3, 2009, involved his "self-dialogue" about risk assessment and the conversation he would inevitably have to have with the first district commander, Rear Admiral Dale Gabel. Gilbert remembered, "I had to prepare myself to answer the question 'why had we launched scarce assets during a storm for what was essentially an ADT alarm?'"[114]

He had fresh information from the aircrew that the flight had been delayed at the air station by "newly fallen snow and darkness" and overheard ship radio transmissions that spoke of "snow showers in the vicinity of the last known position of F/V *Patriot*."[115] He also knew that the rescue chopper had to reduce air speed dramatically, and rescuers had to use night vision goggles in a period of intense snow showers in the search area. Gilbert's thoughts were focused on "putting sailors and aviators lives at risk."[116]

Scarce Rescue Assets

With an area of rescue responsibility that included five Coast Guard sectors from Toms River, New Jersey, to the Canadian border, Gilbert and the district had to manage the single "ready helicopter" and other scarce resources. Gilbert noted, "There were three helicopters for this huge area: one was the ready bird or in 30-minute SAR launch standby, one was in maintenance, and the third aircraft was the 'hangar queen'" (a derisive term for a perennial problem helicopter).[117]

His most emphatic point was that he wanted to dispel the notion that mariners might think the Coast Guard had a fleet of helicopters standing at the ready for every circumstance. The Coast Guard's system needed help from distressed mariners so that the venerable service could manage these scarce resources.

Gilbert also wanted mariners to understand "that for a timely launch, the US Coast Guard search and rescue system is dependent on the mariners themselves; to give some indication of location and the cause of distress. Neither of these were provided to watch standers in the *Patriot* case."[118] He further defended the watch standers, contrary to Papp's report.

SAR CASES ARE A blend of science and detective work.

Speaking to the unique circumstances of the case, Gilbert was doubtful that the Coast Guard watch standers who managed the *Patriot* case had enough information to launch a credible search. Highlighting the fact that they just had a single VMS position and what was essentially a shore-based ADT fire alarm, he considered "the risk of launching the one active helicopter in the district, in adverse weather conditions, with not very much to go on." He further posited, "What if we had launched and found nothing? We didn't really have a searchable area and if we hadn't found the debris field, where would we have then looked?"[119]

Gilbert would further intone that his watch standers had done everything possible by praising their "subsequent investigative work immediately… increased the probability of a vessel in distress, which easily justified the launch."[120]

In the end, Gilbert recognized that his watch standers at every level were grappling with a complex, anomalous case and with a mariner who could not participate in helping define the nature of their distress or where they were. Summing up the situation, Gilbert went on to defend the Coast Guard's actions, "We launched and found wreckage and the deceased victims in the search area. The system worked under very adverse conditions: high seas, freezing cold, snow squalls, reduced visibility."[121]

Challenging the Nature and Completeness of the Report

Gilbert was also concerned that Papp's more formal administrative investigation had further delayed getting answers to the grieving families: "We had completed the District One search and rescue case study and captured the necessary lessons well before Admiral Papp's investigation was concluded." Defending the district and sector watch standers further, Captain Gilbert was also skeptical that the admiral's report did not mention that the VMS feed to Sector Boston had been down for three days and that was "not a sector issue." He was convinced that this factor would have been a "decisive indicator" and driven the case in the inevitable direction much quicker.[122]

Coast Guard Deserves Credit

Days after the government issued its report and coming from an unlikely source, the *Gloucester Daily Times* gave the Coast Guard credit for Admiral Papp's report: "While the conclusions will likely be small comfort to Matteo Russo's widow, Josie, and other family members left behind, perhaps they can draw some comfort from the review of the incident, with recommendations that could result in better SAR operations in the future." In an opinion piece titled "Coast Guard Deserves Credit for Honesty; Now Let's See Change," the paper noted, "Papp certainly deserves credit for a meticulous review of what happened and an unflinching review of what went wrong."[123]

Unanswered Questions

While Admiral Papp's detailed nine-thousand-word report criticized his own service for failure to launch SAR resources for two hours and twenty-three minutes, family members still wanted more answers. Papp would go on to give an interview in *Commercial Fisheries News* and paint a bullseye on "poor coordination and decision-making regarding *Patriot*'s status."[124]

But the admission of the Coast Guard's failure to respond faster was only additive to the pain of losing loved ones, and it did nothing to answer critical questions. Why had a well-maintained boat like *Patriot*, with two fishermen with several decades of experience and at least ten means to communicate their distress, sunk so quickly and catastrophically such that there was no time to don cold-water immersion suits or get in a deployed life raft?

The families would go on to spend tens of thousands of dollars conducting underwater dive surveys and designing plans to refloat the *Patriot*, possibly facilitating more intrusive forensics in order to answer the central question: Why? The government would only approve a detailed safety plan that was exorbitant and well beyond the Orlando and Russo families' means. So, the *Patriot* remains in one hundred feet of water, lying on its starboard side.

The government would try to answer the question in its Marine Casualty Investigation that would be published twenty months after the sinking and fourteen months after VADM Papp's SAR report. The exhaustive report would answer many of the family's questions, but not all. Insights into the *Patriot* tragedy would come from a review of several past search and rescue cases.

Could This Happen Again?

Almost twelve years to the day in 2021, I was back in Coast Guard Base Boston's training room, the same venue that Captain Kulisch had invited me to for a "hot wash" in the 2009 aftermath of the *Patriot* tragedy. Not much had changed physically, except for the blue government-issued face masks everyone wore because of COVID-19.

The walls were still painted the same drab government color—something to do with productivity and sound dampening. The room's fluorescent lights gifted a familiar harsh and unforgiving brilliance even after transitioning from an unusually bright March afternoon sun. But the atmosphere was ironically and pleasantly different and upbeat.

I'd been invited to Sector Boston as an author and search and rescue expert to have a discussion with the 2021 commanding officer, Captain Eric Doucette, and members of his senior staff. Doucette and I had become fast friends during my time as the FEMA Region 1 Administrator from June 2019 to January 2021. I approached Eric about the possibility of interviewing key staff members for this book, at least one who had been present at the command but not directly involved in 2009 when the *Patriot* sank.

I was overwhelmed when Captain Doucette and eight other staff members showed up and talked for more than two and a half hours. They had a good story to tell. More than anything else, they wanted the *Patriot* families to know that they acknowledged the Coast Guard's earlier mistakes and had made drastic cultural and procedural changes. They also let me know there was still a hell of a lot more work to do.

Captain Doucette wanted the families to know that the Coast Guard's relationship with the City of Gloucester and the fishing community had been strengthened over time. He had even brought Chief Warrant Officer (CWO4) John Roberts, the commanding officer of Station Gloucester, to the meeting as testimony to their transparency and openness about my new book. Gloucester was also taking the relationship to a new level and was pursuing an application to obtain status as a "Coast Guard City."

THERE'S JUST TWENTY-NINE COAST Guard Cities that have been recognized since 1998 for "making special efforts to support local CG personnel by acknowledging the professional work of the Coast Guard men and women assigned to their area."[125]

The approval process is onerous and does not authorize any support from the Coast Guard in preparing the extensive application. While Gloucester's application to the Coast Guard Commandant has been delayed by the COVID-19 pandemic, the city hopes for approval "in time for their Quadricentennial anniversary in 2023," noted Captain Doucette.[126]

If approved, Gloucester would join two other Massachusetts cities—Newburyport and Hull—that have achieved status as Coast Guard Cities. Exploring the relationship further, CWO4 Roberts opined that Gloucester's mayor, Sefatia Theken, is a "key player in the relationship

Gloucester Fishermen's Memorial plaques. *Author's collection.*

with the Coast Guard." He also noted that the fire and police chiefs are also very supportive, and that the city has a near-shore search and rescue plan that they exercise with the Coast Guard. Gloucester also has a retired Coast Guard chief petty officer who "works for them and backs us up during rescue cases," Roberts noted.[127]

The Coast Guard operators uniformly praised the relationship with the Gloucester Fishermen's Wives Association (GFWA), led by Angelina Sanfilippo. GFWA, founded in 1969, "has been a strong voice expressing the concerns of the fishing industry at local, state, federal, and international meetings and hearings,"[128] according to its website. Gloucester Station CWO4 Roberts chimed in, "Our relationship with GFWA is right where it should be."[129]

If the GFWA can be characterized as the fishermen's political advocate, the Fishing Partnership (FP) organization is the support services element that coordinates important safety-related courses. The FP hosts two-day sessions twice each year, teaching fishermen about firefighting, stability, use and care of life rafts, dewatering pumps, flares, storage and donning of survival suits, boat maintenance, CPR and first aid. CWO4 Roberts noted, "Coast Guard Station Gloucester hosts the FP training and we're glad to do so."[130]

How would today's Coast Guard respond to another *Patriot* case?

It was a simple question that would occupy most of our remaining time together. Using the Coast Guard's several poor performance areas from Vice Admiral Papp's June 2009 investigation enabled us to have a focused discussion.

Vice Admiral Papp's investigation, the media and later congressional inquiries would address why senior search and rescue decision makers were asleep at critical moments of the *Patriot* case. When I asked the 2021 Sector Boston staff if key senior Coast Guard decision makers would again be seeking "authorized rest" today as they were during critical moments of the *Patriot* case, Jay Woodhead, the Sector Boston senior SAR controller, said, "There are always at least three watch standers available and on watch; and sometimes four during the day."[131]

But Woodhead reminded me that despite the added numbers of watch standers, "The situation with command duty officers being authorized to sleep at some point in a twenty-four-hour watch has not changed."[132]

While the added numbers are important, he felt the most important and substantive change that has occurred and what is different today is that there is a "more mature and forward-leaning culture." Woodhead further explained that Coast Guard search and rescue watch standers now begin with the question, "Is there any reason we shouldn't be going out?"[133]

Additionally, when cases are being evaluated, every watch stander, regardless of level, can drive the logic (positively) and advocate on behalf of the people who may be declaring a distress. In other words, while ultimate decision-making may still be hierarchically driven, the critical thinking on each case is equally divided among the participants regardless of rank or experience. Woodhead also let me know that Coast Guard senior SAR officials are "brought in within ten minutes without question" if there is any ambiguity in a case or if help is required.

Addressing the Experience Factor

Much was said about the three 2009 watch standers during the case who had a "combined experience in their duties at Sector Boston of two years three months"[134] (total), with the most experienced watch stander accounting for twenty-three of those twenty-seven months. It was clear from the case forensics that unlike their apprentices, when more experienced people were awakened and became involved, they made decisions immediately and without hesitation on behalf of the *Patriot* and its crew.

So, how would a *Patriot* scenario play out in 2022? The senior staff at the sector wanted me to know they'd rapidly ramped up their capability during complex cases as a result of more mature organizational constructs.

A Different SAR Organization

Before 2006, the Coast Guard's operational response and prevention pieces were administered by two different units in the same geographic area. The level of cooperation and synergy varied among the predecessor organizations depending on the relationship between the two staffs and their commanding officers.

After 2006, these two commands were fused and became one with the new sectors being established under a single commanding officer. Marc Sennick, Captain Doucette's chief of response, noted, "At the time of the 2009 *Patriot* case, the sector concept was in an early stage of development. Coast Guard stations had lost their autonomy to launch SAR resources and were viewed as an extension of the sector." Sennick went on to indicate that today's stations or any other subordinate unit of the sector "would not hesitate to launch if they believed it appropriate."[135] In other words, the 2022 Coast Guard Station Gloucester officer in charge is, in fact, in charge and would be able to take independent action for a vessel in distress within fifteen miles of the unit.

Additionally, the sector senior staff indicated, "There is a protocol that enables the sector response side to rapidly integrate and expand their capabilities with prevention personnel and expertise."[136] While this might address the numbers, what about all those phone calls and conversations that overwhelmed the 2009 sector watch standers?

A New Type of Efficiency in Sharing Situational Awareness

I thought Captain Doucette was answering an urgent operational matter at this point, but in fact, he was accessing something called the Blue Force Locator on his smartphone. The Blue Force Locator system allows credentialed and authorized parties to instantly pull up pictures of the Automatic Information System (AIS) that was, for example, tracking the tug *Gulf Service* in 2009 and the VMS that provided hourly updates on the *Patriot*'s movements.

Additionally, Doucette said, "The modern Sector Command Center distributes a 'Virtual Morning Brief,' daily at 8:00 a.m. The brief includes a 'snapshot' of Vessel Monitoring System, and additional slides indicating status of all Coast Guard resources, planned operations, and commercial activities. The VMS snapshot has become a routine briefing mechanism shared daily, with the ability to be electronically transmitted to senior officials indicating the status of the fishing fleet. VMS is now routinely utilized to track the fishing fleet's status while flying storm tracks and monitoring the fleet's return to port during winter storms."[137] Storm tracks are Coast Guard flights launched ahead of heavy weather to broadcast storm warnings to offshore vessels.

Doucette clarified that today's sectors have near real-time information in a common operating picture (COP) that is seamlessly sent to all officials to make more informed decisions daily and during heightened operations. The Coast Guard COP tracks fishing vessels, commercial vessels and Coast Guard forces, as well as partner agencies such as the Massachusetts Marine Patrol.

According to Doucette, "Effective use of technology has removed the need for the vast majority of phone calls needed a decade earlier, and enabled multiple levels of leadership to make more informed decisions."[138] Captain Doucette and all the members in the room had the ability to view the same information on their smartphones.

Protocols and procedures for Vessel Monitoring System testing and access had been adjusted in February 2009 at the direction of Vice Admiral Papp, the Atlantic Area commander. Now, at the beginning of every watch, watch standers are required to test their access to VMS and log that test in the chronological record. And if there are difficulties accessing the system at any time, there is a protocol that requires watch standers to shift to the next senior command's VMS within five minutes. There are several watch standers on each shift at each command who now have access to the VMS; it is no longer a question of which watch stander has access to VMS—now most have access.

So, what about the pesky forty phone calls that the 2009 senior sector watch stander had to administer to during the early stages of the case? These calls had left no time for critical thinking, much less analysis. Were they still a problem?

WISE USE OF SMARTPHONES

Holding his phone up for me to see, Captain Doucette assured that today's watch standers would make and receive fewer phone calls if another *Patriot* case occurred. He opined, "We've developed text 'blast lists' that are mature and well-defined and are used to keep appropriate parties in the loop." More than just robust lists of partners who will receive the information, the sharing includes enhanced content such as imagery from the Search and Rescue Operations program (e.g., graphics of intended search tracks), VMS, AIS and coastal camera systems.

There are different blast lists for different types of operations that are unique to the geography where the action is occurring. For example, a law enforcement operation, planned or otherwise, in the Boston Harbor area has a different partner text distribution list than a similar operation near Gloucester.

In other words, there will be fewer partner agency calls because the Massachusetts Marine Patrol, Massachusetts Port Authority, local fire and police departments and other agencies are tied in appropriately and updated simultaneously. By updating one another and receiving and providing information through technology, there's more time for our watch standers to think about the case.[139] The current level of data management sophistication is such that all relevant partners can be dynamically updated about a rescue case while still keeping track of which fishing vessels are responding to advance storm warnings.

When asked for an example where multiple partners were brought together quickly for a complex situation after sharing information through text blast lists, Captain Doucette referred me to a July 11, 2018 case involving the M/V *Sanctuary*. Boston Harbor Cruises (BHC), which oversees *Sanctuary*'s activities, reported a suspicious passenger on the vessel's whale watching trip forty miles east of the city.

BHC reported, "A passenger attempted to board without showing his ticket and was evasive when contacted by crewmembers. He then went to a secluded position in the bow pulpit, did not engage with any persons near him and stared ahead, not paying any attention to breaching whales."[140] The individual was also wearing clothing inappropriate for whale watching activities and carrying a satchel that the crew was afraid might have contained explosives or other threats.

The modern-day Sector Boston commander wanted me to know that "the seventeen agencies and the master of the M/V *Sanctuary* that were involved were well informed and knew what they were looking for with this possible active shooter case." Pictures were sent to all agencies simultaneously. The concept of operations and risk and safety assessments were briefed remotely as the M/V *Sanctuary* was directed to head toward its home port, and law enforcement agencies converged on the vessel.

With law enforcement boarding and search and rescue plans (in case any passengers were to jump overboard if operations went "sideways") in place, the multiagency boarding team embarked the whale watching vessel. They then swept the areas of the boat where the suspicious individual had been known to frequent and interviewed him. While he exhibited "multiple incidents of suspicious behavior," he was transferred to responding officers from the Boston Police Department who met the vessel at the pier. Boston

PD indicated the suspicious individual was held for subsequent medical evaluation after all 249 passengers had disembarked the vessel without interruption.

Work Yet to Be Done

The last forty-five minutes of our time was focused on frustrations felt by members of Coast Guard professionals in terms of programs and laws related to commercial fishing vessel safety. The goal of the Coast Guard's commercial fishing vessel safety program is "to achieve a significant reduction in the Commercial Fishing industry fatalities and vessel losses through public awareness, voluntary dockside examinations and at-sea-boardings." With the passage of the Commercial Fishing Vessel Safety Act of 1988, the program's chief aim is to "foster public awareness of fishing vessel safety and promote regulation compliance."[141]

The goal of these safety boardings is to enable the Coast Guard to enforce U.S. laws and regulations. These include, but are not limited to, fisheries, safety and environmental laws and regulations. Less than six months before the sinking, Coast Guard Commercial Fishing Vessel Safety examiners conducted a voluntary dockside examination of the fishing vessel *Patriot* on July 31, 2008. According to the Marine Casualty Investigation, "No deficiencies were found, and a fishing vessel safety examination decal was issued."[142]

Five months later and less than two months before the sinking, while *Patriot* was underway on a fishing trip, team members from the Coast Guard Cutter *Hammerhead* came onboard. For commercial fishing vessels like the *Patriot*, these boardings included a check of life preservers, the life raft and its equipment, satellite EPIRB, distress signals, fire extinguishers and stability information and instructions. Again, according to the Coast Guard Cutter *Hammerhead*'s report, "No violations. NMFS observer onboard."[143]

At the time of the sinking, the Commercial Fishing Industry Act of 1988 did not mandate a dockside examination for the *Patriot*. It was not until 2010 that additional safety standards, including a mandatory examination, "once every five years, for F/Vs that operate beyond 3 nautical miles," became required. In November 2008, Coast Guard examiners observed the fishing vessel *Patriot* "listing approximately 15–20 degrees to its starboard side while at the dock."[144] The report stated that a *Patriot* crewmember had not aligned the valves correctly and the fuel had become unequally distributed.

COMMERCIAL FISHING VESSEL BOARDING REPORT	BOARDING DATE (MM/DD/YY) / /	BOARDING TIME (24-HOUR)	ACTIVITY NUMBER

VESSEL TYPE: ☐ Fishing ☐ Fish Tender ☐ Fish Processing Vessel VESSEL TYPE CODE:

VESSEL NUMBER	VESSEL NAME

HULL IDENTIFICATION NUMBER	VESSEL MAKE

VESSEL MODEL	YEAR	PROP. TYPE ☐ Outboard ☐ Inboard Gas ☐ Manual ☐ Inboard Diesel ☐ Inboard/Outboard ☐ Other (specify)

LENGTH Ft. In. | NET TONS | HP | HULL TYPE ☐ Aluminum ☐ Fiberglass ☐ Steel ☐ Wood ☐ Other (specify)

FLAG

CFVS DECAL #
DATE ISSUED (MM/YY): /

ENGINE COMPARTMENT: ☐ Open ☐ Closed POBs PFDs
FUEL COMPARTMENT: ☐ Open ☐ Closed
CONSTRUCTION: ☐ Open ☐ Closed

OWNER'S NAME (Last, First & MI) ☐ Mr. ☐ Ms.
☐ Owner was Operator
☐ Owner on Board, Not Operator
☐ Owner Not On Board

STREET ADDRESS/MAILING
TELEPHONE (with area code)
( )

CITY, STATE & ZIP CODE
FEDERAL FISH PERMIT #

DRIVER'S LICENSE NUMBER & STATE | SOCIAL SECURITY NUMBER - - | BIRTH DATE (MM/DD/YY) / /

OPERATOR'S NAME (Last, First & MI) ☐ Mr. ☐ Ms.
TELEPHONE (with area code)
( )

STREET ADDRESS/MAILING
OPERATOR PERMIT #

CITY, STATE & ZIP CODE
FISHERY PLAN CODE:

DRIVER'S LICENSE NUMBER & STATE | SOCIAL SECURITY NUMBER - - | BIRTH DATE (MM/DD/YY) / /

OBSERVED IN USE: ☐ Inside Boundary Line ☐ Outside Boundary Line
☐ Inland Nav. Rules Apply ☐ COLREGS Apply
LATITUDE:

BODY OF WATER: | LOCATION: | ACTIVITY: | LONGITUDE:

REQUIREMENTS FOR ALL VESSELS (Fishing Vessels with a current CFVS Decal: Check items in blue)

140	Life Preservers & Other PFDs	46 CFR 25 & 28.110	141	Ring Life Buoys	46 CFR 28.115
142	Survival Craft	46 CFR 28.120	143	Stowage of Survival Craft	46 CFR 28.125
144	Survival Craft Equipment	46 CFR 28.130	147	Distress Signals	46 CFR 28.145
148	Emergency Position Indicating Radio Beacons (EPIRBs)	46 CFR 25.26 & 28.150, 47 CFR 80	149	Fire Extinguishing Equipment	46 CFR 25.30 46 CFR 28.155 & .160
176	Materiel condition ☐ SAT ☐ UNSAT M00 Follow up recommended		177	Stability/Stability Instructions	46 CFR 28.530 & 46 CFR 28.65 (b) (5)
105	Sound Producing Device	33 USC 2033, Rule 33	138	Backfire Flame Control	46 CFR 25.35
139	Ventilation	46 CFR 25.40-1	145	Lifesaving Equipment Markings	46 CFR 25 & 28.135
146	Maint/Insp of Lifesaving Equipment	46 CFR 28.140	150	Injury Placard	46 CFR 28.165
151	Waste Mgmt Plan (oceangoing vessels>40ft)	33 CFR 151.55 & .57	152	Marine Sanitation Devices	33 CFR 159.7
153	Copy of Nav Rules (inland waters only)	33 CFR 88.05 46 CFR 28.225	154	Navigation/Anchor Lights Sunset/Sunrise (24-Hour)	33 USC 2020 & 2026 Rules 20 & 26
155	Oil Pollution Placard (vessels ≥ 26 ft)	33 CFR 155.450	156	Garbage Placard (vessels ≥ 26 ft)	33 CFR 151.59
157	FCC SSL	47 CFR 80.405	158	Load Line Certificate	46 USC 51
159	Vessel Numbering & Registration	33 CFR 173 46 CFR 67.121 & .123	173	Document/Official Number	46 CFR 67
199	Other				

REQUIREMENTS FOR DOCUMENTED VESSELS OPERATING BEYOND THE BOUNDARY LINE OR W/ MORE THAN 16 POBs

168	High Water Alarms	46 CFR 28.250	171	Instructions, Drills & Safety Orientation	46 CFR 28.270
160	Fireman's Outfit & SCBA	46 CFR 28.205	161	First Aid Training & Equipment	46 CFR 28.210
162	Guards for Exposed Hazards	46 CFR 28.215	163	Navigational Information	46 CFR 28.225
164	Compasses & Deviation Tables	46 CFR 28.230	165	Anchors & Radar Reflectors	46 CFR 28.235
166	General Alarm System	46 CFR 28.240	167	Communication Equipment	46 CFR 28.245 & .375 33 CFR 26.03
169	Bilge Pumps, Piping & Dewatering Systems	46 CFR 28.255	170	Electronic Position Fixing Devices	46 CFR 28.260
172	Emergency Instructions	46 CFR 28.265	199	Other	
178	Coaming Height	46 CFR 28.560 (b)	179	Deadlight Covers	46 CFR 28.560 (f)
180	Non US Master Violation	46 USC 12110 (d)	181	75/25 Crewing Standards	46 USC 8103
119	Negligent/Gross Negligent Operation	46 USC 2302	120	Intoxicated Operations	46 USC 2302 (c)
174	Fisheries Violation(s)		175	Unsafe Conditions -- Terminated Use	46 USC 4505
182	No Violation		183	Law Enforcement Action Taken	

DIST.	UNIT	PHONE NUMBER	BOARDING OFFICER'S NAME (Print)	RANK/RATE

DEPARTMENT OF TRANSPORTATION
UNITED STATES COAST GUARD
CG-4100F (Revised 10/02)

BOARDING OFFICER'S SIGNATURE

NOTE: See reverse side of this page for instructions on processing violations. **BOATING SAFETY HOTLINE (800) 368-5647**
ALL PREVIOUS EDITIONS ARE OBSOLETE
OPERATOR COPY   PAGE 1

The Coast Guard 4100 form (Page 1) for commercial fishing vessels that *Patriot* satisfactorily completed with a boarding team from CGC *Hammerhead* shortly before the sinking. *U.S. Coast Guard sources.*

With the collaborations with the City of Gloucester and the Gloucester Fishing Partnership and the twice-a-year training hosted at the Coast Guard station, the fishing public's awareness was and remains solid and a model set of practices. By all accounts, Matt Russo and John Orlando were not only good fishermen but also safety conscious from an equipment standpoint. They had the required safety equipment, multiple radios, two satellite EPIRBs, cold water immersion suits and a risk avoidance mentality when it came to large ship traffic.

The CFVS Program versus the Cause of the *Patriot*'s Sinking

The Coast Guard's report specified that the *Patriot* had "most likely capsized at 1:12 a.m. on January 3, 2009, leading to rapid down flooding through her open fish hold and engine room hatches and, subsequently, the vessel's sinking."[145] In other words, during the *Patriot*'s retrieval of its last fish haul, the vessel had become unstable to the point where it quickly and catastrophically rolled over with minimal warning.

So, if the *Patriot* and its crew were fully compliant with all safety equipment carriage requirements as well as with all three components of the Coast Guard's CFVS program (public awareness, voluntary dockside examinations and at-sea boardings) that were in place or occurred prior to the sinking, what else could Matt Russo have done to prevent a capsizing?

Analysis: Human Error

The Coast Guard's Marine Casualty Investigation (MCI) pointed to three possible areas of concern related to possible human error. The report noted, "With no surviving witnesses, any actions and decisions taken by either crewmember that contributed to the sinking…are unknown."[146] The MCI would, however, highlight three "known errors" that possibly contributed to the sinking: "the decision to get underway late at night, the decision to get underway with only 2 out of 3 crewmembers, and the use of a controlled substance."[147]

The *Patriot* had gotten underway several times at night and with two crewmen prior to its last voyage without any problems according to those who knew the crew and their routines. The Coast Guard acknowledged the past practice but focused on the third crewmember's duties, which included "checking and maintaining machinery operations, equalizing the port and starboard fuel tanks by means of a crossover valve that allowed the fuel in each tank to maintain levels for stability.…The remaining two crewmembers would have had to fulfill these responsibilities in addition to their own and may have been distracted from an emerging problem on board."[148]

In a March 5, 2009 letter from lawyer Joseph Abromovitz, who represented the Russo family, he indicated "to the best of Mrs. Russo's knowledge the only medication that Mr. Russo was taking at the time of his death were prescription medications." These were prescribed for "Mr. Russo shortly before Christmas [2008] because of an accident he had." The Coast Guard's Marine Casualty Investigation would note, "The use of a controlled substance could have negatively affected the alertness of the crew and prevented them from reacting to an emerging situation."[149]

CHANGES AFTER THE *PATRIOT* SINKING

The Coast Guard Authorization Act of 2010 and the Coast Guard and Maritime Transportation Act of 2012 established additional safety and equipment requirements for commercial fishermen. However, only one requirement actually took effect, according to the Sector Boston staff: the "mandatory examination, once every five years, for fishing vessels that operate beyond 3 nautical miles."[150] Even these five-year dockside exams have significant shortfalls when viewed through the *Patriot* lens, squarely focused on stability issues.

LACK OF LICENSING

Coast Guard members continue to be stymied by the lack of licensing for those who occupy one of the nation's most dangerous occupations, reflecting on the fact that "a launch tender operator who is limited to going 1,000 feet offshore has more (government) scrutiny for their qualifications than commercial fishermen."[151] There is no effective way to enforce safety standards for boats that go two hundred miles offshore that can be manned with people who have no experience, no licensing and no enforcement. A Sector Boston staff member noted that a "Commercial Driver's License for a dump truck driver provides more fidelity than what exists for a much more dangerous commercial fishing vessel industry."[152]

Others I spoke with said, "The financial situation of most fishermen continues to be cost-prohibitive for necessary and voluntary stability tests that routinely run between five and fifteen thousand dollars."[153] The Coast Guard inspectors present noted that even "without formal licensing, you hope that the Engineers on commercial fishing vessels have the capability to manage a boat's problems and load stability (e.g., balancing fuel loads)."[154] But as we all know, hope is not a planning factor on which to rely in a deadly serious occupation.

The *Sea Farmer II* Incident, October 20, 2020

The Boston Sector staff wanted me to know of a recent example of how a lack of experience and standards for licensing adversely affected one fishing vessel's voyage. At about 2:45 p.m. on October 20, 2020, Boston Sector's northern counterpart, Sector Northern New England, headquartered out of South Portland, Maine, was contacted by the owner of the seventy-five-foot trawler *Sea Farmer II*. The owner reported that the vessel's generator had failed during a fishing operation when the boat was sixty-five miles east of Portsmouth, New Hampshire.

The *Sea Farmer II* was able to make slow speed using its twelve-volt battery power, but the generator failure meant the batteries would quickly drain. A Coast Guard patrol boat was dispatched to tow the boat to the nearest safe harbor.

Once the towing operation began, the batteries ran low and the vessel lost power to its auxiliary systems, including its onboard distress communications radios, computer navigation and steering systems, as well as its ability to retrieve its deployed nets. When the boat was closer to shore, the owner and a mechanic were transferred to the vessel to complete repairs of the generator.

The Coast Guard's report indicated that the "generator failed due to improper maintenance procedure conducted by an inexperienced crewmember."[155] Further investigation determined that earlier in the day, the boat's engineer found that the oil pressure gauge on the generator was flickering in the engine room.

Normally, the generator required three and a half gallons of lube oil for proper operation. To address the flickering light and what he believed to be low lube oil pressure, the engineer proceeded to add approximately *seven* gallons of oil. The generator shut down due to excess oil in the cylinders.

The Coast Guard report went on to note a "failure to provide training to a crewman in order to complete maintenance on the engine room equipment" as a causal factor. And a "latent unsafe condition existed that degraded the crew's readiness onboard to respond to routine or emergency procedures."[156] The master of the vessel stated that he had "difficulty finding qualified crewmen to staff his fishing boat."[157]

After five days of repair work on equipment and in the engine room, the boat owner went on to note, "It was difficult to find out exactly what was going on," because "commercial fishing vessels should be required to have an independent communications device separate from the ship's power." The *Sea Farmer II* was fortunate that there had been a National Marine Fisheries Service observer onboard at the time of the incident. In a November 26, 2020 letter to the Coast Guard, he lamented, "If it were not for the observer's satellite device, I would not have known how dire the situation was."[158]

THOUGHTFUL CONSIDERATIONS

Even after this extraordinary briefing and discussion, I was left wondering if this sector, this group of extraordinary professionals, was typical of the entire Coast Guard search and rescue organization. Or were they a bright, shining star group of serious professionals led by an extraordinary leader? Had all of the lessons learned from the *Patriot* case been inculcated service-wide, especially in the Coast Guard's bread-and-butter search and rescue mission?

6

ANATOMY OF SEARCH AND RESCUE MISSIONS

The 2009 *Patriot* case was not the Coast Guard's first use of the fisheries law enforcement Vessel Monitoring System in a search and rescue circumstance. Eight years before the *Patriot* sank, the search for the fishing vessel *Starbound*, with several Gloucester fishermen aboard,[159] was assisted by the Coast Guard using locating information from VMS off the coast of Maine, with a very different outcome.[160]

Why did the Coast Guard employ VMS information in the 2001 *Starbound* case when it stumbled with the same system for the 2009 *Patriot* case? Insights would come from an analysis of how the venerable rescue service was alerted by *Starbound*'s rescue emergency, which was very different from the *Patriot*'s situation. The specifics of the *Starbound* case would highlight how and why *Patriot* rescue personnel were stuck in analysis paralysis, unable to move forward until "after two hours and twenty-three minutes of fact finding."[161]

Just after midnight on August 5, 2001, the fishing vessel *Starbound* was run down by the 541-foot Russian oil tanker *Virgo* approximately 130 miles east of Cape Ann, Massachusetts, in dense fog. The tanker *Virgo* was northbound, headed for its next port of call at Come by Chance, Newfoundland.

Starbound was trawling southbound for fish and maintaining an active watch for other vessels. James Sanfilippo, thirty-six, from Gloucester, Massachusetts, was at the fishing vessel's helm. As the tanker *Virgo* appeared suddenly out of the fog and bore down on the helpless vessel, collision was imminent and Sanfilippo screamed to his fellow crewmen that the small fishing vessel was about to be rammed and they needed to quickly don their survival suits.[162]

Captain Joseph Marcantonio, also from Gloucester, had gone below to sleep when he awoke to Sanfilippo's urgent call. A Coast Guard investigator, Lieutenant Soliz, recalled Marcantonio "saw a tanker or freighter—a large ship—bearing down on them on the port side."[163] There was no time, and it was a "matter of seconds before the collision occurred."[164] Marcantonio leaped up the three steps to the pilot house, inquiring, "What's the matter?" Sanfilippo said, "What the fuck, what the fuck!" Marcantonio looked forward to see "what was putting that look of horror on his face. What I saw was a large bulbous shape rolling towards us, plowing through the sea."[165] The fishermen, alerted by Sanfilippo's cries, scrambled from below to don immersion suits to protect themselves from the sixty-six-degree water and sought their way to the safety on the deck of the vessel.

Marcantonio would tell investigators that the port side of the fishing boat scraped along the length of the tanker, the forward hull of the fishing boat collapsing. David Hench from the *Portland Press Herald* would lament, "The *Starbound* had no time to change course and the crew no time to get out."[166] Marcantonio, the only survivor, told the Coast Guard that *Starbound* sank in less than ten seconds.

Both he and Sanfilippo could "see the water, a huge black welter of it, churning and spitting as it came bulging up the galley way." Marcantonio saw "a black column of water shoot out the galley way as though it had been fired from a cannon."

Marcantonio swam away from where *Starbound* sank and found the boat's life raft. The fortunes of luck were with the boat's captain as he settled himself and retrieved the vessel's hydrostatically triggered satellite EPIRB, a device intended to float free and alert rescue agencies that help was urgently needed.

The visibility was about one to two miles as Marcantonio watched the *Virgo* quietly recede into the shroud of darkness. The seas were calm, and local fishing vessels reported an occasional rain squall. *Virgo* made no course or speed changes and no effort to assist *Starbound*. An eerie quietude descended on the lone survivor.

The boat's captain repeatedly called out to his crew from the life raft, but no answers came back. Marcantonio had last seen Sanfilippo in the *Starbound*'s pilot house.

The Coast Guard would not get *Starbound*'s position from the initial satellite EPIRB alert and would have to wait for a second satellite pass about forty-five minutes later to receive accurate locating information. Rescuers also attempted to employ the Automated Mutual Vessel Reporting (AMVER), a system designed to track participant ships oceanwide and communicate with vessels near a distress case.

In a search and rescue training session in January 2009, a Coast Guard briefer reported that AMVER had 3,422 vessels registered and "reported their positions to the Coast Guard on a daily basis to lend assistance in an emergency."[167] In a slide titled "Merchant Ships to the Rescue," a lone mariner is shown being hoisted aboard a merchant ship and saved from certain disaster.[168]

The Russian ship *Virgo*, although its track was registered in the AMVER system, did not respond to the Coast Guard's repeated calls to alter course to help the *Starbound*. And so, *Virgo* continued on its journey to Come by Chance, Newfoundland, oblivious to the deaths of four fishermen and having violated no less than five International Navigation Rules and Regulations.[169]

Starbound's Captain Joe Marcantonio later told authorities the impact of the collision felt like a car wreck. Rear Admiral George Naccara, U.S. Coast Guard (Retired), then the Coast Guard's District One Northeastern commander, commented that he doubted a vessel the size of *Virgo* would have felt the impact with the smaller fishing vessel. He also indicated that the Russian ship should have seen the fishing vessel on radar or visually.[170]

Coast Guard rescuers determined the *Starbound*'s last known VMS geographic position immediately after receiving the initial EPIRB alert. The satellite EPIRB system would require a second orbit and about forty-five minutes to pinpoint the beacon's location, so knowing approximately where the *Starbound* had been from its VMS position immediately gave a searchable starting point and enabled the mobilization of aircraft to begin heading toward a specific search area.

By 1:45 a.m., the Coast Guard had launched an HU-25 Falcon jet that would quickly find a debris field and the EPIRB's flashing strobe light. Marcantonio was rescued four hours after the sinking by a lobster fisherman in the fishing vessel *Eulah McGrath* who recovered the severely hypothermic and shivering Marcantonio from his raft and returned him to that vessel's homeport in New Hampshire.

The lifeless body of *Starbound* fisherman James Sanfilippo of Thomaston, Maine, was found early on the day of the collision by another fishing vessel, the *Jacqueline Robin*, but the bodies of fellow crewmen Mark Doughty, thirty-three, of Yarmouth, Maine, and Tom Frontiero, forty, of Gloucester, Massachusetts, were never recovered. The question remains: how did the Vessel Monitoring System help the Coast Guard in the *Starbound* case?

Starbound's VMS position was calculated in the general vicinity of the (eventual) EPIRB's distress beacon location, thereby providing a second verification of the fishing vessel's EPIRB distress homing beacon. The major difference between the successful 2001 *Starbound* rescue case and the 2009 *Patriot* case was that in the older case, rescuers were alerted and triggered into immediate action by a traditional satellite EPIRB distress alert from the distressed vessel; in the *Patriot* case, there was no standard alerting Mayday tripwire for the Coast Guard.

In the 2001 *Starbound* case, rescuers correlated the presence of VMS locating information while *Patriot* rescuers struggled with a nontraditional boat fire alarm, the plea for help from the co-owner and the total absence of traditional reports of distress (e.g., EPIRB, VHF-FM, flares).

What made the *Patriot* case difficult for watch standers to act on a precise last known position provided by the VMS and the call from the co-owner and wife? What were the differences between the *Starbound* and *Patriot* cases and the watch standers' thought processes?

The 2001 *Starbound* case was a textbook bright-line distress case where rescuers were quickly activated and motivated by an affirmative traditional alerting system (satellite EPIRB). In the forty-five minutes between the initial EPIRB alert and a later satellite pass that determined accurate position information, *Starbound*'s last VMS position gave rescuers an aim point or last known position to start their planning to send rescue resources.

In the 2009 *Patriot* case, there were no traditional search and rescue clues other than the co-owner's fervent pleas for help. This was a case that required aggressive advocacy and problem-solving skills that were not resident among the junior watch standers.

Doctrine at the time of the *Patriot* case told watch standers that VMS was "merely a tool to assist with fisheries law enforcement, homeland security, and search and rescue.…VMS is a valuable search and rescue *forensics* tool, allowing the controller to step back through time to see not only the last position of a VMS equipped vessel, but also to see which VMS equipped vessels have transited the same basic area as the potential distress case" (emphasis added).[171]

So, why did the Coast Guard not put Josie Russo's 1:35 a.m. call for help together with the absence of the *Patriot* VMS (and cellphone, EPIRB, VHF-FM) alerts? Why did they work so hard *not* to advocate for the *Patriot* crew and waste time sending land crews to the Gloucester pier to check out the anomalous fire alarm? The answers are not with technology or additional watch personnel but rather are more insidiously nascent to every watch stander and in understanding human behavior—and organizational culture that exists even today, thirteen years after the *Patriot* sank.

How did the Coast Guard exclude the possibility that another *Heather Lynn II* tragedy had occurred with the *Patriot* being overrun by a tug and tow? If the *Patriot* had been hit by a heavy barge, it would explain the sudden nature of the tragedy and give certainty to the grieving Russo and Orlando families. If it wasn't a collision, what happened on the *Patriot* during its last hours, minutes and seconds that would create a circumstance that doomed two seasoned mariners so quickly that they could not get off a distress call, put on their cold-water immersion suits or climb into the boat's life raft? The insight to answers came from a variety of sources, technologies and partnerships, some new, some old.

What happened on the *Patriot* to cause it to rapidly sink if the tug *Gulf Service* did not run over the boat? Russo and Orlando family members wanted definitive answers and spent tens of thousands of dollars on their own investigative efforts. Despite both crewmen likely drowning within minutes of the sinking and before Josie Russo's first call for help, the Coast Guard's own rescue miscues would cast serious doubts on the venerable service's analyses.

Critical to the Coast Guard's *Patriot* investigation were data collected from bottom-tethered buoys used to monitor critically endangered North Atlantic right whales (*Eubalaena glacialis*). The information was gathered from a conservation program sponsored by NOAA, the Woods Hole Oceanographic Institution and Cornell University. With fewer than 350 left, right whales were so named because they were the "right" whales to catch, since they floated when killed by the whaling community in past centuries. These days, leading causes of right whale mortality are from ship strikes and entanglements in fishing gear.

Dr. Peter Tyack of the Woods Hole Oceanographic Institution researches social behaviors and communications of large sea animals. He said that researchers position buoys in the approaches to Boston Harbor, which intersect known right whale transit areas. These buoys capture sounds, perform analysis and relay the information about nearby whales in near real time so that the government can issue Notices to Mariner broadcasts and route ships away from these animals.

Tracking and analyzing unique sounds of North Atlantic right whales happens through a series of buoys that capture large amounts of data over prolonged periods. To identify, locate and document the distribution of North Atlantic right whales, Marine Autonomous Recording Units

A forty-one-foot U.S. Coast Guard utility boat monitors movements of an entangled whale near Provincetown, Massachusetts. *Used with the permission of the* U.S. Naval Institute Proceedings *magazine.*

(MARUs) were deployed in Massachusetts Bay over five years starting in October 2008. This was the same area where the *Patriot* sank. The MARU buoys were fabricated in a cooperative effort by the Cornell Bioacoustics Research program in Ithaca, New York.[172]

The government and partner nongovernmental organizations (NGOs) track the whales' seasonal movements to understand their habits and migration patterns, warn mariners in near real time and eventually shape maritime law to preserve their numbers and limit harmful interactions with humans. It's this technology that helped pinpoint the *Patriot*'s last movements and moments.

The Coast Guard made good use of the buoy data. "Four of the nineteen buoys were not recording on the night of January 2 due to a malfunction. Eight functional MARU buoys were located within 10 nautical miles of the F/V *Patriot*'s wreck location with two of the functional buoys located within 5 nautical miles," the report stated.[173] The data from the buoys came in individual data files that were fifteen minutes long, each buoy having a separate channel. According to the Coast Guard's 2010 investigation, "The time stamps on the files are calibrated to GPS time. The buoys which captured the *Patriot*'s sinking were deployed from October 11, 2008, to January 21, 2009."[174]

In a 2011 *Soundings* magazine article, journalist Jim Flannery wrote, "Taking a cue from the high-tech sleuths on television's 'CSI,' the Coast Guard has used underwater audio recordings from 19 acoustic whale-tracking buoys to help reconstruct the sinking of the fishing vessel *Patriot*." Those same buoys that could record marine mammal sounds could also capture the "sounds of engines and props of nearby boats." The novel effort would require multiple agencies to cooperate in new ways, including "the Navy's super-secret undersea surveillance office in Virginia Beach, Virginia," according to Flannery.[175]

The relationships brokered by the Coast Guard, the Navy, the private sector, NGOs and academia would eventually help resolve whether the fishing vessel *Patriot* had been either "overtopped" by the tug *Gulf Service*'s heavy towing hawser that connected the tug and its following barge or run down by the barge. Overtopping is when a vessel is caught between the tug and towed barge and the heavy towing hawser catches on some part of a fishing vessel such as a trawl door or Gallus frame and drags it underwater or overturns it.

In a number of cases, warnings are not enough, and whales become entangled in, are injured and often die from run-ins with fishing gear. Each submarine and marine mammal has unique underwater sound characteristics, as does each fishing boat and vessel that passes near these underwater hydrophones, including the fishing vessel *Patriot* and tug *Gulf Service*. Recordings from the buoys would provide investigators a trove of information.

To establish a baseline of "normal" sounds from the fishing vessel *Patriot*, previous boat noises from a December 2008 fishing trip were pulled off the MARU hydrophones for various boat operations (e.g., engine noises while transiting, engine noises during speed changes while fishing, motor noises for hauling back fishing nets, wash down pump noises, etc.). These countless noises from the previous trip became the "*Patriot* reference sound profile" or baseline of sounds for what was normal and uniquely identified the boat from all other boats—an audio fingerprint, in essence. The same process was followed for determining the unique sound signature for the tug *Gulf Service*'s engine and equipment noises, based on past trips near the buoys.

The sounds for *Patriot*'s normal operations could then identify this particular fishing vessel among all other craft and be compared with the sounds that happened during the night of January 2 and the early morning hours of January 3, 2009, before and during the accident. Similarly, the routes (courses and speeds) and noises in the early morning hours for the *Patriot* and the tug *Gulf Service* could be determined accurately by interpolating what scientists and Navy technicians call the Time Difference on Arrival (TDOA). TDOA, as explained by Cornell's Dr. Chris Clark, is like standing close to a railroad bridge and listening as a train approaches, passes and recedes. On the night of January 2 and the morning of January 3, 2009, *Patriot* boat machinery and equipment noises arrived at the different MARU buoy locations at slightly different times, enabling sophisticated Navy algorithms to determine what was going on aboard the vessel, where it was and what its course and speed were, moment to moment. A similar analysis of sounds was undertaken with the tug *Gulf Service*'s unique noises that were received at the different bottom-mounted MARU buoys on the night of the accident.

These sound difference times on noise arrivals, coupled with the *Patriot*'s traditional VMS and the *Gulf Service*'s AIS tracking information, were then translated into precise ship tracks, including time, position, course and speed. This information, in the composite, would determine if another 1996 *Heather Lynn II* (a tug's barge colliding with a fishing vessel) had occurred with the *Patriot* and tug *Gulf Service*.

Since 2004, the International Maritime Organization has required all commercial vessels greater than 299 gross tons (e.g., tug *Gulf Service*) to be equipped with AIS Global Positioning System tracking systems for various uses, including avoiding collisions and monitoring maritime traffic.[176] The tug *Gulf Service*'s AIS historical data for the night of January 2–3, 2009, was archived and quickly reviewed by the Coast Guard within forty-eight hours of the sinking.[177]

The *Patriot*, on the other hand, was equipped with NOAA-required VMS—a system that fishermen derisively referred to as "government ankle bracelets"—mandated for the type of fisheries in which the vessel was involved. The *Patriot*'s VMS pinged the vessel's position at least hourly and randomly within each hour to inhibit fishing vessels encroaching on closed fisheries' areas in between pings. Both AIS and VMS systems had accuracies to less than three hundred meters.[178]

As part of the Coast Guard's investigation, they determined which vessels came near the *Patriot*'s last VMS ping at 12:30 a.m. on January 3 and narrowed the list down to a few nearby fishing vessels that were well to the north, and the transiting tug *Gulf Service* and its barge, containing Number 6 fuel oil. The *Gulf Service* was rapidly identified as a possible target for further investigation to determine if a collision had occurred.[179]

The timing, courses, speeds and positions from the various technologies could then be used to determine how close tug *Gulf Service* and the *Patriot* came to each other before, during and after the accident. *Patriot*'s last VMS ping would be recorded at 12:30 a.m. at a position approximately fourteen nautical miles east of Gloucester. Mariners are always alert to collisions at sea and routinely plot all nearby vessels with radar in order to determine the closest point of approach (CPA). Most captains define critical thresholds and want to avoid close CPAs.

The combined Navy and Coast Guard analyses determined that the tug *Gulf Service* and its barge *Energy 11103* towed 1,300 feet astern "transited through the immediate area and passed within approximately 2.5 nautical miles of the *Patriot* at 12:01 a.m."[180] But no closer. If the *Gulf Service* and its barge were not the culprit, what happened onboard the *Patriot* after midnight? The underwater sounds were unremarkable and normal for a typical fishing trip to Middle Bank. That is, until around 1:12 a.m. At that time, the first and last retrieval of a fish haul, the buoys detected the *Patriot* flooding and eventually hitting the bottom less than ten minutes later.

Part III
PERSPECTIVES

Semper Paratus (Always Ready)
The Official Coast Guard March
by
Captain Francis Saltus Van Boskerck, USCG (1928)

We're always ready for the call,
We place our trust in Thee.
Through howling gale and shot and shell,
To win our victory.
"Semper Paratus" is our guide,
Our pledge, our motto, too.
We're "Always Ready," do or die!
Aye! Coast Guard, we fight for you.

7

TENSIONS

M arch 2009. A few months after Russo and Orlando died, the notoriously strained relationship between tugboat captains and the Gloucester fishing community was keenly evident in a bitter early morning exchange over VHF radio on March 28, 2009. The backstory is that Gloucester fishermen loathed tug operators. The fishermen's latest theory was that the southbound tug *Gulf Service* with its tow might have interacted with the *Patriot* on the night of January 3, 2009, maybe even caused its destruction. And so, the fishermen's narratives were not friendly toward tugs and their towed barges.

A LONG NIGHT FOR TUG *MERIT:* MARCH 27, 2009

About 11:30 p.m., the tug *Merit* departed Boston Harbor, bound for Newburyport with a 160-ton construction crane in tow. Aboard were Captain Dave Desmond; Captain Greg Bashaw, *Merit*'s second skipper; and Dominic Orlando, a deckhand and son of John Orlando. The weather wasn't too bad—a light breeze flitted across the surface. Captain Bashaw recalled that they had waited almost two weeks for the right weather to haul the crane to Newburyport. Today was the day, with a small sea state forecasted.[181]

Dominic enjoyed a brief break and recalled he was "relaxing on the tug's construction boom"[182] as they chugged along. He remembered that bats had taken up residence in the boom and were flying about, and the evening wasn't that cold. As expected, within minutes the tug cleared Boston Harbor and headed northwest. Then, the weather started to worsen.

Swells from the southeast ambled up the tug's side. Friction from pounding waves snapped a critical wire towing hawser cable between the tug and barge. Captain Bashaw and Dominic Orlando rigged a "softer," flexible mooring line. A good tug captain is ready for any variation from the norm. Tug *Merit*'s 40-foot by 130-foot barge and its crane had briefly been towed astern when leaving the pier to provide greater maneuverability. Now, the barge would be maneuvered and pushed ahead of the tug to provide better control.[183] Unfortunately, moving the barge to the pushing position in front of *Merit* blocked the tug's radar—a difficult and dangerous tradeoff especially at night or in reduced visibility. Captain Desmond indicated that *Merit*'s radar "was obstructed, but only in a small sector directly ahead of us and we would regularly maneuver the tug left and right of track to make sure we could see ahead of us on radar."[184]

Around 4:40 a.m., fog settled in. Captain Bashaw spoke to the skipper of the tug *Miles Andrew*, which was heading out of Beverly Harbor to the north, and told him that "visibility was dropping and towing conditions were sloppy."[185] Bashaw slowed the *Merit* to three to four knots. Orlando was the tug's lookout, posted forward on the barge. He could see beyond the construction crane and was armed with a sledgehammer to bang on the barge's deck to make noise and warn any nearby ships or boat traffic of their presence. Captain Desmond recalled that Orlando was "on the barge with a hand-held VHF radio. He was close enough that I could yell to him if necessary."[186]

Meanwhile, Bashaw initiated timed security calls—standard protocol in dangerous sea conditions—between 5:00 and 6:00 a.m.—to warn nearby vessels about the reduced visibility and their presence. At 5:06 a.m., the tug *Miles Andrew*, alerted by Captain Bashaw's security broadcasts, stayed near shore where visibility was better. The tug *Miles Andrew* would eventually link up with tug *Merit* near Cape Ann after transiting the Annisquam Canal System, an area notorious for fishing vessels crisscrossing from the east towards the fishing grounds.

This day was no exception. Bashaw's report indicated, "A couple times we had to make course corrections to avoid vessels that were headed eastbound."[187] Fog wrapped the *Merit* as the dawn light began to rise off Gloucester. Visibility was low, but the water was flat calm. The sun's warming effect had thinned the fog. Local seas were littered with fishing boats from

Gloucester. Just then, the VHF radio on the bridge popped to life. Vitriol directed at Captain Bashaw bellowed from the speaker. "You f——— on the tug—cutting right through the fishing fleet and grounds. You ——— on tugs trying to kill us—just like what you did to the *Patriot*! Are you ——— kidding me coming through here at 10 knots cutting us off!" Tempers boiled.

To the fishermen's defense, the Gloucester community was still recovering from the loss in 1996 of the F/V *Heather Lynne II*, the vessel that came between a tug and its tow in which the heavy wire towing warp overturned the fishing vessel, thirteen years before the *Patriot* sank.[188] The tug *Houma* and its 272-foot barge ten miles off Cape Ann, Massachusetts, ran down *Heather Lynn II*. *Houma*'s barge weighed over 1,250 tons and was connected to the tug by a thick wire cable of over 1,000 feet in length and a heavy chain bridle. While *Heather Lynn II* had been physically struck and run over by the *Houma*'s barge, fishing vessels knew that they only needed to come between the tug and barge, and the cable itself would have enough inertia to flip over and sink a relatively small fishing vessel. Kate Yeomans, author of *Dead Men Tapping: The End of the Heather Lynn II*, likened the 1996 collision between tug and tow and the fishing vessel to "a truck and plow" with the towed barge being "more than 400 times the weight of the fishing vessel."

Still, for Dominic Orlando, the raw rebuke from members of the Gloucester fishing family and analogy to fresh wounds made time stand still. The men on the two fishing vessels involved with tug *Merit* in the verbal altercation could not have known that John Orlando's son, Dominic, was working with his friend Captain Greg Bashaw that day as part of the tug's three-person crew. Dominic relived his worst nightmare of losing his father, John, two months earlier.

Those aboard the fishing boats could not have known that Captain Greg Bashaw had been asked by the Orlando and Russo families to help them unravel the mystery of the *Patriot* sinking a short while after the tragedy. Bashaw was surprised that the family asked "if there was any point where there would be a possibility of a collision (with the tug and tow)."[189] Bashaw helped the family plot the *Patriot*'s hourly Vessel Monitoring System positions and the tug *Gulf Service*'s Automatic Information System tracking locations. Bashaw's earlier interactions with the *Patriot* families, plus Dominic Orlando being onboard as a deckhand for tug *Merit*, put the late March 2009 encounter with the Gloucester fishing vessels off the irony chart.

Bashaw's later report to the Coast Guard noted that at 6:30 a.m., the *Merit* had slowed to between two to three knots, and "we could just make out two fishing boats on our port side. One was a black hulled vessel, forward and further away from us. The other was white hulled and closer to our barge on the port side." Bashaw had heard the boats conversing on Channel 72 VHF beforehand, and he was confident the 120 feet of steel on boom of the construction crane they were pushing made a "fine radar target, if they [the fishing vessels] had been using radar."[190] Both fishing vessels were showing the day shapes/signal for fishing with trawl gear, but they did not have their running lights on."[191]

Mariners are required by the U.S. Coast Guard Navigation Rules to display lights during reduced visibility that uniquely identify their activity. Fishing vessels actively fishing must display lights (or day shapes) that are different from the lights they display if merely transiting. Similarly, the tug and tow would have been displaying lights for a vessel restricted in its ability to maneuver and to reflect the length of the tow.

Reacting to the presence of the two fishing vessels, Captain Desmond said that he "put the boat in neutral and reverse and stopped the barge within one vessel length. This enabled both the fishing vessels to pass across our bow from the port to the starboard side. Once past, we continued back on our course of 315."[192]

Captain Desmond noted that "the fishing vessels' gear was on their net reels. They were not hauling back or trawling. In the simplest terms, those Gloucester fishermen crossed in front of us without stopping or giving way as they were required to by the Rules of the Road. We stopped, let them pass ahead of us."[193]

A Different Viewpoint

Captain Bashaw saw things differently in the early morning hours of March 28, 2009, and later filed an incident report with the U.S. Coast Guard. Bashaw noted, "We are headed North, and the [fishing] boats were coming out of Gloucester and they are headed East toward the fishing grounds. We were not 'in the fishing grounds' area, and they were not fishing yet. They were power vessels headed East."[194]

Captain Bashaw was asserting that since the fishing vessels were transiting and not actively fishing that they should have yielded to tug *Merit*, a vessel restricted in its ability to maneuver. Bashaw's interpretation of the encounter was 180 degrees out from the fishermen's viewpoint. "I talked to the guy on the radio afterwards and told him, 'We were doing 3 knots at best and if he could get the tug *Merit* to go 10 knots under any condition, I'd give him a million dollars.'"[195]

In Bashaw's view, the fishing vessels were supposed to give way to the tug *Merit*, a vessel constrained in its ability to maneuver, according the International Collision Regulations, or the rules of the road for ships at sea. Captain Bashaw is referring to the *2014 US Coast Guard Navigation Rules & Regulations Handbook*, part of a 1972 international treaty adopted by Congress in 1977 in order to avoid collisions at sea. Rule 24 applies to the *Merit*, and Rule 26 applies to the fishing vessels.

He was further flummoxed by the circumstance because the fishing vessels were operating in dense fog "without running lights" as required at the time of the vessels' encounter. Fisherman Mike Leary, who worked these same waters for more than a decade, observed that "not once from my time between 2003–2013 did I see them [Gloucester fishermen] with the proper lights."[196]

Gloucester Daily Times reporter Richard Gaines, himself a fisherman, further dramatized the close encounter in an article shortly afterward: "A tug…operating without radar emerged from a 'black thick of fog' just past Thacher [*sic*] Island into a flotilla of day-fishing boats, local fishermen said yesterday."[197]

According to Bill Lee in the fishing vessel *Ocean Reporter* and Paul Theriault in the fishing vessel *Terminator*, they were trawling for the "spring influx of haddock with the federal closing of the inshore waters just days away at the end of the month."[198] Theriault indicated he had barely avoided a collision by throwing his motor into neutral and giving the winch full power.

The *Gloucester Daily Times* article continued, "This action caused the boat—which has less drag than the net and trawl doors on the bottom—to tend to slide backward briefly, just enough to allow the 130 foot-long, 40-foot-wide barge, pushed by a 30-foot tug, to ease past."[199]

"The situation was made worse by the fishermen not monitoring the required distress frequencies, channels 13 and 16 VHF. And only coming up on channel 16 after the close encounter,"[200] said Bashaw. Title 33 CFR 26 provides the regulations for vessels to monitor certain radio channels and frequencies in order to ensure safety at sea.

Fisherman Bill Lee recalled the decisive moment very differently, "Out of the fog it comes—aiming right for Paul Theriault's *Terminator*. He tries to call him [the tug] on channel 16. Everybody is listening and watching and all of a sudden the tug changes course and turns towards me, and I said, 'No way he can avoid hitting me.'"[201]

Lee went on to indicate, "It was a bad situation. Paul is asking their intentions, there was no response on the radio, I grabbed a life jacket, he [the tug] had a choice of hitting him or hitting me." But somehow, tug *Merit* did not hit either the *Terminator* or the *Ocean Reporter* and "vanished into the fog," according to Lee.[202]

Lee was further angered "when I tried to call the tug on Channel 16, the Coast Guard came on, and they were scolding me to tell me I wasn't hailing or in distress. I can't talk to the captain of the tug while he's bearing down on me?"[203]

Interviewed twelve years after the incident, Dominic Orlando didn't think much of the situation with the fishing vessels at the time. "We could clearly see the fishing vessels and they could see us and it wasn't a big deal. After the *Gloucester Daily Times* article came out, I was in a charity poker tournament with Billy Lee, and he started talking up the story and I got so mad and flipped the table on him. The whole thing was ridiculous."[204]

The mystery of a tug and tow in the *Patriot* case would be resolved some fifteen months later when the Coast Guard exonerated *Gulf Service* using unusual scientific-based methods and procedures normally reserved for hunting and tracking enemy submarines—and whales. The Coast Guard knew a tug and tow had been in the area of the *Patriot* on the night of the sinking, but how could they verify one way or another that the fishing vessel had been struck by the tug and tow? Did the fishing vessel *Patriot* suffer the same demise as the ill-fated fishing vessel *Heather Lynn II*?

Within hours of the *Patriot*'s two crewmen being recovered, the Coast Guard shifted the case from recovery to the forensic investigation to answer the question, "What caused the boat to sink so quickly?" Matt Russo and John Orlando, seasoned mariners with more than forty years of combined fishing with positive safety records, were found deceased in the water, both partially clothed and without their survival suits on. Fellow fisherman friend Mike Leary knew that Captain Russo was cautious about "larger vessels, freighters, tugboats, and would always call on the radio [channel 16 VHF-FM] sometime as far away as six miles to make sure the bigger boats knew the fishing boats were also in the area and engaged in fishing."[205]

Jay Woodhead, now Sector Boston's Lead Command Center controller, was at home the day after the 2009 *Patriot* sinking when he heard about the case on the local news. Woodhead recalled immediately "reviewing the AIS/VMS historical plots for the evening in question. That early track review for the *Patriot*'s area of operations indicated the tug *Gulf Service* had operated near the accident."[206]

The local Gloucester fishing community would embrace the tug-and-tow narrative for several months. A bullseye would be painted squarely on this theory and cause at least one family member of the *Patriot* crew ironic angst just a few months after the sinking. Until the Coast Guard finished a series of investigations, no one would know anything for certain.

8

REFLECTIONS

Three Coast Guard admirals placed themselves on the record about the *Patriot* case. The first to do so, within weeks of the sinking, was the First Coast Guard District commander, Rear Admiral Dale Gabel. Gabel was an engineer by trade and a Coast Guard "cutter man," having spent more than a decade on four different ships, including command of a high-endurance cutter. When Gabel assumed command of the First Coast Guard District in Boston, he was a seasoned senior officer and had been a flag officer for more than six years. Admirals in the sea services are called flag officers because each is authorized to fly a special flag denoting their military rank. Admiral Gabel was the first to address the families and the Gloucester community, well before any investigations were concluded. Gabel would place the Coast Guard visibly on the record despite conventional wisdom suggesting that it would be politically safer to let junior field commanders speak about difficult cases.

WHY DID MY NEWSPAPER DO THAT?

Within days of the sinking, Admiral Gabel had penned a six-hundred-word letter to the *Gloucester Daily Times* "expressing condolences to the families and explaining that the Coast Guard would carry out an evaluation of all aspects of the *Patriot* case."[207] The fact that the *Gloucester Daily Times* had printed the admiral's entire letter in the opinion section drew criticism from the paper's constituency, causing editor Ray Lamont to rationalize its publication in his own piece titled, 'Why Did My Newspaper Do That?'[208]

Lamont admitted, "In most cases, an admiral offering any comment on a fishing boat tragedy that claimed the lives of two local fishermen might only be used in a news story, and would have been issued as a press release. And in those cases, we might have printed just a few lines of the full statement in a news story while also getting back to others involved in the story for their reaction."[209]

The paper, Lamont conceded, had printed stories in the preceding days that included comments from the fishing community, and discussion focused on the Coast Guard's response and the investigation. More importantly, the editor wanted his readership to know, "the Opinion page—offers the best chance for the Coast Guard, or anyone else, for that matter, to communicate with Gloucester and Cape Ann's residents on a large scale."[210] Lamont praised Admiral Gabel for choosing the most direct route to address the local fishing community and their families as opposed to presenting his letter on Boston-area TV or radio, "so he chose—right so, I'm proud to say to send the letter to the local community newspaper where readers could check it out and review it several times over."[211]

Eight months later, Rear Admiral Sally Brice-O'Hara, the Coast Guard's deputy commandant for operations, testified in front of the House Committee on Transportation and Infrastructure. This committee had oversight over the Coast Guard and many aspects of transportation safety.[212]

Brice-O'Hara brought extensive operations-ashore experience to the congressional table having been a field commander and deputy field commander at multiple shore units with search and rescue (SAR) responsibilities. She began her testimony with a recap of the previous year's SAR statistics, indicating, "In 2008, the Coast Guard prosecuted over 24,000 SAR cases, saved 4,910 lives, and assisted an additional 31,628 people in distress."[213] Heralding a 2007 milestone, she mentioned the Coast Guard having celebrated its millionth life saved.

Brice-O'Hara's seven-page introductory statement would go on to recap search and rescue improvements in capability, including "the creation of the Coast Guard Sectors, places with demonstrated experience and sound judgment in critical leadership positions." She also spoke about rapidly advancing information technologies such as improved SAR planning software, and Rescue 21, the enhanced near-shore VHF-FM communications system, applicable to where 90 percent of Coast Guard rescues occur.

Brice-O'Hara added that the introduction of 406 MHz direction-finding equipment on Coast Guard aircraft improved "the overall performance of our SAR capability."[214]

Highlighting the complexities of rescue work, Brice-O'Hara lectured that even with the best of technology, "search and rescue remains a mixture of art and science. A SAR case is impacted by human factors ranging from initial reports by anxious or panicked mariners to judgment calls by Coast Guard personnel working under the most pressing circumstances. The sea remains an unforgiving place.…Unfortunately, lives are going to be lost."[215]

Admiral Brice-O'Hara mentioned the term "bias for action" twice in her remarks. In her summation, she said, "We ingrain bias for action in every recruit, officer candidate, and cadet; every Auxiliarist and civilian watch stander; indeed, every member of Team Coast Guard."[216] As if a ball had been teed up, Congressman and Subcommittee Chairman Elijah Cummings, D-Maryland, responded to the admiral's generalizations about improved capabilities with a specific comment related to the *Patriot* case and suggested otherwise: "This is not some hypothetical; this is real stuff."[217]

In the subcommittee's own session briefing paper the members noted that both the sector and district command duty officers "were asleep at the time of the incident," conditions that "may have played a role in the relatively inefficient processing and analysis of case information."[218] Reacting to the congressman's inference that junior watch standers delayed in seeking help from their more experienced seniors, Brice-O'Hara admitted that "we have to instill within watch standers a complete sense that any question, any need for assistance in standing their watch tautly and properly, should never be something embarrassing."[219]

Gloucester Reacts

Brice-O'Hara conceded that "training and orientation of duty officers needed improvement." She also said that the "*Patriot* case will be imbedded in our training."[220] In an editorial that followed shortly after the admiral's testimony, the *Gloucester Daily Times* noted, "Nothing can erase from many people's memories that, when time was of the essence, the US Coast Guard responded in anything but a timely and effective manner."[221] Brice-O'Hara would not be the last Coast Guard admiral to comment on and contextualize the *Patriot* case. Admiral Robert Papp, now promoted to a four-star flag officer, would be installed as the service's twenty-fourth commandant on May 25, 2010. He came onboard with a single-minded purpose: to address institutional problems in basic areas.

The new commandant had inherited significant "symptoms of cultural and leadership challenges" that would see him attending funerals for nine Coast Guardsmen who died in the line of duty during his tenure.[222] Admiral Papp saw an opportunity to take a breath and get back to basics. One of his inaugural emphasis areas was to "do everything I could to course correct and make improvements and Steady the Service."[223]

The Cost of Pet Projects

Papp had seen some of his predecessors "pursuing new initiatives in the absence of authorization and resultant follow-on funding from Congress." Each of these pet projects brought with them major course changes for the Coast Guard that required new resourcing, doctrine, procedures, and training. Papp knew that paying for unfunded self-imposed initiatives came in the form of taxing the budget models of downstream operational units and often cost both money and time.

These taxes ultimately took away from professional training. In several notable cases, he had seen previous commandants' "big ideas" get started and either never get finished or take years to come to fruition because proper Congressional processes in the form of Coast Guard Authorization Acts (which would codify the changes and prompt budgetary action) were not accomplished.

As if to confirm his strategic concerns for past tax-and-pay programs, Papp witnessed Coast Guard operational tragedies that had exposed serious flaws in training and leadership. Immediately prior to becoming the commandant, the admiral was the chief of staff for the Coast Guard and was responsible to sign off on administrative investigations, "take action" and in some cases brief the families of those who had died.[224] One case in particular caused him to frame his future foci as the new commandant.

Divers Died as Party Went On Above

So announced a January 13, 2007 article that ran in the *Seattle Times*. The headline sprang from an administrative investigation that followed the deaths of two Coast Guardsmen on August 17, 2006. Five hundred miles north of Barrow, Alaska, two Coast Guard divers descended from the nearby icebreaker *Healey*. The purpose of the dive was to familiarize two new divers and prepare them for future cold-water immersions. These dives are sometimes necessary to check the underwater hull of a ship that routinely clears a path by driving its reinforced bow area up onto the ice pack—and crushing it with its weight. This highly technical dive was supposed to be for a short period and only to a twenty-foot depth.

Contrasting with the seriousness of an Arctic dive in twenty-nine-degree water, the ship's captain had authorized alcohol to be brought on board the cutter contrary to Coast Guard policy and metered out during an "afternoon party with alcohol, an ice football game, and 'polar bear' swims."[225] Polar bear swims in cold water with minimal clothing are designed to enhance crew morale. Nothing about the cold-water dive would enhance crew morale.

Dissecting Disaster

Admiral Papp and his staff would forensically analyze the cutter *Healey*'s leadership climate from the moment the mooring lines had been taken aboard in Seattle until after the accident. He would recall that at least one officer with "oversight responsibilities for the technical dive operations had consumed six beers" despite the ship's captain having directed that no crewmember should consume more than two beers. He also recalled there was a "bidding war for those personnel who had an extra beer or two from their two-beer maximum."[226]

Within seconds of entering the water, both Coast Guard divers' tending lines began to pay out fast like big fish on the *Wicked Tuna* reality TV show. One of the cutter's safety line-tending support team members, who "had been drinking beer moments before,"[227] had to place his foot on the spool to prevent it from running away.[228]

Forensics indicated that the two safety lines had been deployed to depths beyond 180 feet and, in one case, 220 feet. Once the seriousness of the divers' situation was suspected by the shore safety personnel, the unresponsive divers were retrieved. Both divers were declared dead within hours, despite receiving immediate medical attention from the ship's complement.

The twenty-seven-page administrative investigation highlighted "numerous departures from standard Coast Guard policy at various levels despite the availability of policy that would have prevented the loss of life." The report faulted a lack of oversight of the cutter's dive program and a failure to use a system of risk management that would have "provided a sound check on the timing, necessity, value, and risk of this dive."[229]

The investigation focused on the divers who "lacked an adequate combination of training, experience, and judgment to recognize and properly manage the high risk of cold-water diving and failed to follow known procedures and regulations."

The report bashed program management of the service's dive program, indicating it had not "kept pace with the growth of Coast Guard missions following the terrorist attack of 11 September 2001." Noting that the number of dive units had increased from five to seventeen over the past five years, "There has been no growth in dive program management or training billets, or in their seniority to accompany expansion."[230] The final action memorandum would mandate that the dive program be elevated on par "with other high risk, training intensive operations such as aviation."

Coupling the *Healey* deaths with a number of other recent avoidable Coast Guard boat and aviation tragedies rooted in procedural and human behavioral flaws, Papp would contextualize the *Patriot* case within larger organizational challenges he inherited.

Patriot: Another Symptom of System-Wide Concerns

With regard to his experience with the Gloucester case, Papp said, "*Patriot* didn't shock me. It was another indicator of the problems our service had been experiencing over the last decade." Taking aim at the project to create the sector organizational construct that had begun more than a decade before, he lamented the experience gaps that were evident.

Papp recalled, "Command centers used to be manned with loads of experienced personnel. We used to send seasoned cutter commanding officers from eighty-two- and ninety-five-foot patrol boats to command centers; they all had four to six years' experience, and that operational time gave them a sense of urgency." Reacting to the paucity of experience and training the Sector Boston *Patriot* watch standers had, Papp was pensive, saying, "I never blamed them, because they didn't have the experience or proper training."[231]

The Genesis of the Operations Specialist Rating

One of the past commandant's projects that Admiral Papp alluded to in his "tax-and-pay" comment was the Joint Ratings Review (JRR). The JRR was a Coast Guard working group chartered by three directorates in headquarters: the operators, the technologists and the workforce administrators. Begun on May 20, 1997, the effort was designed to "examine enlisted ratings responsible for the maintenance and operation of non-aviation electronic systems." Their goal was to "posture the workforce to best maintain and operate equipment used to accomplish missions of the Coast Guard out to the year 2010."[232]

The initial team's work was concluded before the summer of 1998, but it would take years to effectively "merge the Electronic Technician (ET) and Fire Control ratings into the new ET rating; merge the Boatswain's Mate (BM) and Quartermaster rating into one BM rating; create a new Information Systems Technician rating; and create an Operations Specialist (OS) rating."[233]

Enlisted performance qualifications for the new ratings had to be developed. New training courses had to be created, including the hiring of curriculum development support. New advancement cycles had to be defined, as well as standards for how service members were evaluated for the new ratings. These changes took almost four years to define, advertise and begin the implementation process in the 2003 timeframe. Six years later, in 2009, the Coast Guard was still grappling with supplying shore SAR stations, sectors and its cutter fleet with a well-trained and experienced cadre of the new OS rating, the specialty principally tasked with search and rescue.

The JRR was just one of several past commandants' initiatives that Papp saw that needed to be stabilized. The organization needed to take stock and breathe life into what its new commandant referred to as a "new emphasis on mastery of craft and leadership" to ensure the Coast Guard is prepared to "confidently take the initiative in fulfilling its missions."[234]

Admiral Papp would capture his service stabilization platform in an August 2012 U.S. Naval Institute *Proceedings* magazine article that focused on proficiency. The service's chief would go on to describe proficiency in three areas: craft, leadership and disciplined initiative. Each of these "anchor" areas included responsibilities at the individual, unit and organizational levels.

The Three Anchors

Proficiency in Craft. The admiral's first anchor among a triad of new emphasis areas was defined by professionalism within a chosen field. Noting that each Coast Guardsman has a primary professional specialty area where they gain "advanced knowledge, experience and seasoning," Papp articulated a requirement for every individual to develop a self-discipline and an adherence to rules and standards. This self-discipline would not only ensure a safer, more effective work environment but foment a disciplined team. The commandant set an expectation of continuously striving to become better at what they do through "dedication to duty, persistence, and time."[235]

Proficiency in Leadership. The second touchstone area provided for a renewed emphasis on traditional concepts of leadership, highlighting that no matter the size of the organization, "there is always one individual vested with the ultimate authority, responsibility, and accountability."[236]

These commanding officers, officers-in-charge and team leaders have the same opportunity to be lifelong learners within the discipline of leadership that their subordinate specialists pursue. Papp would opine that leadership at every level is important, whether at the small team level, staff level or as a service executive, and must "succeed in thousands of places every day for the Coast Guard to function."[237]

Disciplined Initiative. The commandant's third seminal area focused on leaders at every level being able to "use initiative that is standards-based to conduct the mission." Noting the infectious good nature of leaders who hold themselves and the people they lead accountable within standards, Papp emphasized that this, more than anything, would create a climate of trust. This would be a trust that would extend to every level of the unit and create an environment in which the leader did not need to be present for every mission, knowing that discipline within the standards would inevitably empower initiative.

A Sense of Pride

Admiral Papp would have a great sense of satisfaction when he attended his successor, Paul Zukunft's, change of command in June 2018. Noting that "not a single on-duty death had occurred"[238] in the intervening four years, he took comfort that his previous efforts had helped Zukunft and those who followed *Steady the Service.*

EPILOGUE

Studying rescue watch stander normalcy bias, a human factor behind complacency, could and should be the subject of future Coast Guard analysis. Without an understanding of why rescuers, regardless of experience, become complacent, the Coast Guard will occasionally continue to have lapses in superior service to mariners, sometimes with catastrophic results.

Readers may also be heartened to know that until 2018, when the curriculum was updated, lessons learned from the *Patriot* case continued to be taught at the National Search and Rescue School—a joint initiative by the Coast Guard and Air Force—in Yorktown, Virginia. The course focused on operational decisions that should have been made sooner in 2009, such as how VMS is part and parcel of every rescue profile, for instance. However, no mention of normalcy bias was discussed at the school that carries a mission to provide standardization and professionalism within the search and rescue community.

Prior to COVID-19 in March 2020, and subsequently the Maritime Search and Rescue Planning course going online in early 2020, search and rescue students were taught the *Patriot* case in the Case Studies class in the resident course. Resident courses are physically taught on campus. Having restarted in October 2021, the SAR School brought the Maritime Search and Rescue Planning students back to class (in person) to teach the *Patriot* case. I'm hopeful that normalcy bias will become part of the updated curriculum there. However, COVID-19's Omicron variant may threaten face-to-face learning opportunities that enhance dynamic interactions.

A Boat Owner's Responsibility

In the *Patriot* case, while minimal government standards for the vessel were met or exceeded by the boat's owners and crew, Matt Russo could have done more to lessen his own and his father-in-law's risk profiles. He might have pursued voluntary stability testing, avoided sailing at night and added a third crewmen instead of being underway with just his father in law.

A most profound insight from writing the *Patriot* book and others has to do with a mariner's responsibilities for their own safety, which go beyond the Coast Guard's or even the law's legal minimum requirements for the preparations necessary to participate in fishing, one of the deadliest occupations.

Past Coast Guard commandant Jim Loy spoke about this topic at the U.S. Naval Institute in Annapolis, Maryland, on April 22, 1999, just prior to a search and rescue panel attempting to determine the "value of life." His goal for the speech was to "learn, take stock, and encourage prevention skills for all of us who have parts to play in making or going to sea a safer experience."[239] While his speech focused on a 1997 sailboat accident (*Morning Dew*) that took the lives of a father, his two sons and a nephew, the admonitions to mariners remain relevant in the *Patriot* case and for all other mariners.

I am hopeful that fishermen who read this book consider going beyond the minimum published standards for safety and government requirements. They can contact the area Coast Guard sector for information about stability testing. Indeed, there are several cases in the last forty years in which commercial fishing vessels are thought to have become unstable during routine operations, with catastrophic results.

A longtime friend, Dr. Peter Smith, a psychologist who previously worked with the Coast Guard and now advises emergency service personnel and agencies, suggested "reaching for the stars, engaging other rescue organizations both here and abroad in meaningful dialogue about exceptionally difficult cases and where we or our clients had failed." By the same token, Peter challenged my former service to consider whether it wants to be known as the *premier* maritime rescue service, an elite agency because "nobody does it better."[240] To do so, asking the most difficult questions and conducting self-eviscerating analyses will ensure the likelihood of future *Patriot* cases is minimized.

Smith believes the Coast Guard's approach to normalcy bias should be to ask the question, "what does *Semper Paratus* (Always Ready) mean when something goes wrong, when information is incomplete and other elements

Patriot's wheelhouse. *Used with the permission of GoodmorningGloucester.org.*

One of the plaques containing the names of the more than 5,300 Gloucester sailors who have died at sea. On the plaza near the Gloucester Fishermen's Memorial. *Author's collection.*

LET A PRAYER BE SAID

We'd laugh and play all the day
between his labors at sea.
Now that's changed, my days re-arranged.
He's no longer there for me.

I heard it said, what I did dread,
and feared the long nights through
That a ship was lost at the terrible cost
of her captain and the crew.

What can I say of that tragic day?
What dirge be upon my lips?
Let a prayer be said, for the dead,
They that go down to the sea in ships.

Neil Kleindienst's poem "Let a Prayer Be Said" at the plaza near the Gloucester Fishermen's Memorial. *Author's collection.*

(fatigue, poor staffing, training) are at play?" He hopes this book "gets under the Coast Guard's skin" enough to lead to further "cultural and operational changes." The goal should be a well-trained and equipped SAR system that is "second-to-none."[241]

On February 15, 2009, Gloucester's former poet laureate John Ronan celebrated the lives of Giovanni "John" Orlando and Matteo Russo with a celebratory poem at the Cape Ann Cinema.[242] The poem, titled "The Salt of Gloucester," which is reprinted with Ronan's permission at the beginning of Part I, characterizes the men and the unforgiving sea they charted and paints them as humorous, loving and dedicated fishermen and family men.

He describes the pain and suffering of the families as they balance hope and faith with the inevitable reality of the tragedy. With broader strokes, Ronan casts the lost men as part of a larger Gloucester legacy that includes more than 5,300 other fishermen who have died at sea doing what they loved and were bred to do.

5,300

Matt and John's names have been memorialized alongside over 5,300 other names on a plaque adjacent to Gloucester's Fishermen's Memorial, established in 1923 to honor and commemorate the thousands of fishermen lost during the city's first three hundred years.

Historical records indicate, "In 1879 alone, 249 fishermen and 29 vessels were lost during a terrible storm."[243] The harbor-facing side of the statue is inscribed with bronze raised lettering from Psalm 107:

> *THEY THAT GO*
> *DOWN TO THE SEA*
> *IN SHIPS*
> *1623–1923*[244]

Dedicated in 1925 to thousands of Gloucester fishermen who perished at sea, the iconic Gloucester Fishermen's Memorial or *Man at the Wheel* overlooks Gloucester Harbor. *Author's collection.*

ACKNOWLEDGEMENTS

Many have made contributions, large and small, to this book. Without their wisdom, expertise and generosity, I could not have written it.

I'm grateful to members of the Orlando and Russo families who contributed their heartfelt memories and perspectives: Dominic Orlando, who helped me describe who his father, John, was and humanized the book in many ways with his perspectives and remembrances. He also was with Captains Bashaw and Desmond in March 2009 as a crewmember on a tug and barge being pushed north in dense fog where Gloucester fishermen were upset at the tug and invoked the earlier *Patriot* case in their narrative. And to Salvatore Russo, Matt's brother, thank you. Sal helped me understand who his brother was and what Matt's loss meant to his family and the fishing community. My thanks to Christian Rodolosi, crewman from the *Patriot*. Christian gave the story authenticity of what it was like to fish for cod and enabled the author to understand who John and Matteo were while they were fishing. Christian also provided the perspective of a former Coast Guardsman.

To Commodore Brad Lima, Merchant Marine (Retired), a friend and colleague from our time together at Mass Maritime, my thanks for your nautical counsel and engineering insights.

To retired Coast Guard captains Tom Vitullo and John Kondratowicz for their enduring friendship and advice as the book evolved and became real. Your encouragement will always be appreciated. I'm grateful to Captains Greg Bashaw and Dave Desmond, tugboat skippers and friends to Dominic Orlando, a son of John Orlando. Greg and Dave helped me capture the unique relationship between the commercial tugboat community and the Gloucester fishermen in the months after the accident.

To my aviator hero and friend Rick Bartlett for helping me describe what the Coast Guard helicopter crew experienced during their early morning flight to assist the *Patriot* on January 3, 2009. Rick spent the better part of four decades flying rescue missions for the Coast Guard and the state of Maryland until his retirement in 2021.

Captain Eric Doucette, 2021 commanding officer, Sector Boston, was instrumental in providing access to Coast Guardsmen who helped me understand today's positive relationship between Gloucester and the Coast Guard. And what enduring lessons the Coast Guard has assimilated as a result of the *Patriot* case.

Commander Myles J. Greenway, Sector Boston's Prevention Department head, coordinated all aspects of this author's interface with Sector Boston's staff, and to whom I will forever be grateful for his responsiveness and kindness. Myles leads Marine Safety Operations and executes a captain of the port, officer-in-charge, marine inspection and federal maritime security coordinator role in New England's largest port.

Lieutenant Sam Guinn, National Search and Rescue School, provided much-needed insights on how today's Coast Guard watch standers incorporate past lessons learned.

Commander Marc Sennick, Sector Boston, 2021 response chief, lent understanding as to how the 2009 *Patriot* case lessons learned have been assimilated into watch standers' training and consciousness.

Lieutenant Ryan Cuga, 2021 chief of investigations, Investigations Division chief/senior investigating officer, Sector Boston, helped with a substantial Freedom of Information Act request and provided detailed answers regarding the changes to the Coast Guard's commercial fishing vessel safety program after the *Patriot* case. Ryan is responsible for the tactical planning and execution of investigations for marine casualties and violations of U.S. law and the prosecution of suspension and revocation against mariner's credentials. His civil enforcement actions promote maritime safety.

CWO4 John Roberts, commanding officer, CG Station Gloucester, provided crucial insights regarding the City of Gloucester's relationship with today's Coast Guard.

Jay W. Woodhead, Sector Boston Lead Command Center controller. Jay was present at Sector Boston in 2009 and played a critical role in identifying and deconflicting the tug *Gulf Service* as the culprit in the *Patriot* sinking. He remains the "corporate memory" for all things related to search and rescue.

My thanks to John Buckley, Sector Boston commercial fishing vessel safety coordinator. John leveraged his twenty-eight years of marine safety and technical expertise to greatly benefit the Coast Guard and the Port of Boston. He routinely conducts dockside safety examinations on commercial fishing vessels. He is known as a passionate advocate for vessel and crew safety.

Jim Pritchard, Sector Boston, is the assistant senior investigating officer and assists in the planning and execution of marine casualty investigations. Jim and the other Coast Guard civilian employees are not subject to rotational assignments, and their expertise provides immense stability and benefit to the safety programs that support local mariners.

Chief Warrant Officer Paul Roszkowski, Coast Guard Motion Picture Office, for helping kick-start conversations with today's Coast Guardsmen.

Dr. Peter Smith, longtime friend of the author and contributor in the discussions about normalcy bias and how it affects watch standers and first responders.

My thanks to Dr. Chris Clark, Cornell University, for his help in describing the NOAA Marine Autonomous Recording Unit buoys and their critical role in capturing fishing vessel *Patriot*'s engine and machinery noises throughout this final voyage. These audio recordings were pivotal to the descriptions and narrative of what John Orlando and Matt Russo were doing in their final hours. And to Dr. Peter Tyack, Woods Hole Oceanographic Institution, for giving the author a better understanding of the different buoy systems used to capture and interpret marine animal sounds.

Lieutenant Mike Barker and BMCM Mark Cutter, former operations officer and officer in charge, Coast Guard cutter *Flying Fish*, for their graphic narrative of the chaotic events of the early morning hours of January 3, 2009. Mike left *Flying Fish* to become an officer based on the *Patriot* experience and, with Mark's encouragement, made a real difference explaining the virtues of empowerment in an otherwise checklist-oriented community at the 2010-era Sector Boston command and the Coast Guard Search and Rescue school. *Flying Fish* and its crew exhibited the best of what the guard had to offer in an otherwise dismal performance by our former service.

Captain Andrew White, former Coast Guard officer and friend, for providing insights from his time on VADM Papp's Atlantic Area staff during the development of the SAR investigation. Lastly, I reserve my greatest thanks to Rear Admiral George Naccara, U.S. Coast Guard (Retired), District One commander and leader immediately after the 9/11 attacks, lifetime mentor and now friend, for his continued support and fellowship.

NOTES

Part I. Tragedy

1. John Ronan, "The Salt of the Sea," an email with permissions from the author, September 2021.

1. Time-Honored Routine

2. Morison, *Maritime History of Massachusetts*, 142.
3. Matt Russo's obituary in *Wicked Local*, January 5, 2009.
4. Ibid.
5. Sal Russo, interview with the author, April 17, 2021.
6. Ibid.
7. Ibid.
8. Christian Rodolosi, interview with the author, March 3, 2021.
9. S. Russo, interview, March 2, 2021.
10. Prybot, "Matt's Got a New Boat."
11. Ibid.
12. Ibid.
13. Ibid.
14. Mike Leary, interview with the author, March 8, 2021.
15. NIOSH, U.S. Commercial Fisheries Fatalities. Item obtained from USCG through the Freedom of Information Act process [hereafter FOIA].
16. Leary, interview.
17. Rodolosi, interview, April 1, 2021.
18. Ibid.
19. Ibid.
20. S. Russo, interview, April 17, 2021.

21. Gaines, "Families Push for Underwater *Patriot* Photos."
22. S. Russo, interview, April 17, 2021.
23. Ibid.
24. Ibid.
25. Ibid.
26. Ibid.
27. U.S. Coast Guard [hereafter USCG], *Investigation into the Circumstances Surrounding the Sinking of the F/V* Patriot [hereafter F/V *Patriot* Investigation], 24, 25.
28. Rodolosi, interview, March 3, 2021.
29. BMCM Mark Cutter, interview with the author, April 28, 2021.
30. Mike Barker, interview with the author, June 1, 2021.
31. Ibid.
32. Dominic Orlando, interview with the author, March 17, 2021.

2. The Search

33. Ibid.
34. BMCM Cutter, interview, April 28, 2021.
35. Ibid.
36. Ibid.
37. USCG Station Gloucester Log-Remarks sheet, January 3, 2009, FOIA.
38. John Orlando's obituary in the *Gloucester Times*, January 5, 2009.
39. Rodolosi, interview, March 3, 2021.
40. S. Russo, interview, April 17, 2021.

3. What Happened?

41. Raymond, "What Is Hydrostatically Released Unit."
42. USCG F/V *Patriot* investigation, 3.
43. Captain Greg Bashaw, interview with the author, 2021.
44. Ibid.
45. USCG F/V *Patriot* investigation, 31.
46. Ibid., 33.
47. Ibid.
48. Ibid., 33.
49. Gaines, "*Patriot* Family to Sue Tug Owner."
50. USCG F/V *Patriot* investigation, 32.
51. Ibid.
52. Ibid., 13.
53. Ibid., 15.
54. Ibid.
55. Ibid.
56. Rodolosi, interview, March 3, 2021.

57. S. Russo, interview, April 17, 2021.

58. Sample, "Why Do Submarines Get Caught in Fishing Nets?"

59. Nuclear Policy Info, Microsoft PowerPoint, "Fishing vessel submarine interactions.ppt," https://www.nuclearpolicy.info/wp/wp-content/uploads/2020/07/Fishing_vessel_submarine_interactions.pdf.

60. Ellen Ouellete, from Webster and Webster, *The* Sol e Mar *Tragedy off Martha's Vineyard*, 58.

61. USCG F/V *Patriot* investigation, 26.

62. Ibid.

63. Ibid.

64. USCG Activity Report; MC94018454-F/V *ITALIAN GOLD*, FOIA.

65. Ibid.

66. USCG Sector Boston email to the author, October 25, 2021.

4. Investigations

67. USCG Summary of Statement (with Boston M.E.) form, September 18, 2009.

68. USCG Cold Exposure Survival Models for the victims, undated, FOIA.

69. National Cold Water Safety Center, "Cold Shock."

70. Gloucester Fire Department Dispatch Log, January 3, 2009.

71. USCG, *Final Action on Administrative Investigation of the Coast Guard Response to the Sinking of the F/V* Patriot *That Occurred on January 3, 2009* [hereafter USCG F/V *Patriot* Final Action].

72. Ibid.

73. Rear Admiral Sally Brice-O'Hara, testimony to Congress, September 30, 2009.

74. USCG F/V *Patriot* Final Action.

75. USCG National SAR Addendum, January 2013.

76. Ibid.

77. Ibid.

78. Ibid.

79. Ibid.

80. Rick Bartlett, email to author, September 13, 2021.

81. Ibid.

82. Ibid.

83. Check-six.com, "Fatal Coast Guard Aircraft Accidents"; Burke, "Living Honor Heroic Coast Guard Crew."

84. USCG Commandant Instruction 3500: Risk Management.

85. Bartlett, email to author, September 13, 2021.

86. Ibid.

87. USCG F/V *Patriot* Final Action.

88. USCG Sector Boston Case Log/Chron Sheet, January 3, 2009, FOIA.

89. USCG District One (drm) Memorandum 16130.

90. USCG press release, "Coast Guard Seeks Answers in Patriot Case," January 8, 2009.

91. USCG District One (drm) Memorandum 16130.
92. USCG email, January 7, 2009, Taskers for Commandant Coast Guard.
93. Ibid.
94. "Coast Guard, MSP Owe a Full Probe into Patriot Sinking," *Gloucester Daily Times*, January 7, 2009.
95. USCG F/V *Patriot* Final Action.
96. Ibid., 12.
97. Ibid.
98. Ibid., 13.
99. Justia US Law, US District Court for the District of Massachusetts.
100. Admiralty and Maritime Law Guide, *US v. Hurd and Cornett families*.
101. Ibid.

5. Lessons Learned

102. USCG F/V *Patriot* Final Action, 14.
103. USCG 2013 SAR Addendum, 1–8.
104. USCG F/V *Patriot* Final Action, 14.
105. Gaines, "Coast Guard Steps Up."
106. USCG F/V *Patriot* Final Action.
107. Webster, "Too Tired to Tell."
108. USCG F/V *Patriot* Final Action, 15.
109. Ibid., 15.
110. Ibid., 16.
111. Ibid.
112. Ibid.
113. Ibid.
114. Captain Craig Gilbert, interview with the author, August 17, 2021.
115. USCG Air crew CG 6004 statement to the record detailing their search and recovery on January 3, 2009, undated.
116. Captain Gilbert, interview, August 17, 2021.
117. Captain Gilbert, phone interview, September 20, 2021.
118. Captain Gilbert, email, September 27, 2021.
119. Ibid.
120. Ibid.
121. Ibid.
122. Captain Gilbert, interview, August 17, 2021.
123. "Coast Guard Deserves Credit for Honesty; Now Let's See Change," *Gloucester Daily Times*, June 16, 2009.
124. "CG Acknowledges Short-Falls in Patriot SAR Response," *Commercial Fisheries News*, July 2009.
125. USCG, uscg.mil.
126. USCG Sector Boston staff, interview with the author, March 23, 2021.
127. Ibid.

128. Gloucester Fishermen's Wives Association, gfwa.org.
129. USCG Sector Boston staff, interview.
130. Ibid.
131. Ibid.
132. Woodhead, interview with the author, September 10, 2021.
133. USCG Sector Boston staff, interview.
134. USCG F/V *Patriot* Final Action, 10.
135. USCG Sector Boston staff, interview.
136. Ibid.
137. Doucette, email to the author, August 25, 2021.
138. Ibid.
139. Ibid.
140. USCG Suspicious Activity Report, July 11, 2018.
141. USCG Commandant Instruction 16711.14 dated March 3, 1993.
142. USCG F/V *Patriot* investigation.
143. Ibid.
144. Ibid.
145. Ibid.
146. Ibid.
147. Ibid., 41.
148. Ibid., 42.
149. Ibid., 45.
150. USCG Sector Boston response to draft notes from March 2021 interview.
151. Ibid.
152. Ibid.
153. Ibid.
154. Ibid.
155. USCG *MISLE Incident Investigation Report*; Sea Farmer II.
156. Ibid.
157. Ibid.
158. Sandler Fisheries Inc. letter, November 26, 2020.

6. Anatomy of Search and Rescue Missions

159. Hench, "Hit and Run Ship Sought."
160. Ibid.
161. USCG F/V *Patriot* Final Action.
162. Ibid.
163. Ibid.
164. Ibid.
165. Ciaramitaro and Marcantonio, "Fifteen Years Ago Lives Were Lost."
166. Ibid.
167. Niles, Katherine, USCG, US/USA SARSAT Training Miami Beach, Florida, January 2009.

168. Ibid.
169. U.S. Department of Homeland Security, *United States Coast Guard Navigation Rules & Regulations Handbook*, Rule 7: Risk of collision, Rule 8: Action to avoid collision, Rule 14: Head-on situation, Rule 16: Action by Give-way vessel, Rule 18: Responsibilities between Vessels, Rule 19: Conduct of vessels in restricted visibility.
170. RADM George Naccara, interview with the author, July 5, 2021.
171. USCG F/V *Patriot* Final Action.
172. USCG F/V *Patriot* investigation, 22.
173. Ibid.
174. Ibid.
175. Flannery, "Coast Guard Reconstructs Mystery Sinking."
176. Marine Traffic, "What Is AIS?"
177. USCG Sector Boston staff, interview, March 23, 2021.
178. USCG F/V *Patriot* investigation, 12.
179. USCG Sector Boston staff, interview, March 23, 2021.
180. USCG F/V *Patriot* investigation, 12.

7. Tensions

181. Captain Bashaw, email to the author, May 7, 2021.
182. D. Orlando, interview with the author, March 17, 2021.
183. Captain Bashaw, interview with the author, March 4, 2021.
184. Captain Desmond, interview with the author, May 11, 2021
185. Captain Bashaw, interview, March 4, 2021.
186. Captain Desmond, interview, May 11, 2021.
187. Captain Bashaw, report to USCG, March 2009. Report provided to the author by the captain.
188. The *Heather Lynn II* tragedy was chronicled in *Dead Men Tapping* by author Kate Yeomans.
189. Bashaw, email to the author, May 6, 2021.
190. Ibid.
191. Captain Bashaw, report to USCG, March 2009.
192. Captain Bashaw, interview, March 4, 2021.
193. Captain Desmond, interview, May 11, 2021.
194. Captain Bashaw, interview, March 4, 2021.
195. Ibid.
196. Leary, interview.
197. Gaines, "Close Call for Fishing Boats."
198. Ibid.
199. Ibid.
200. Ibid.
201. Ibid.
202. Ibid.

203. Ibid.

204. D. Orlando, interview with the author, May 5, 2021.

205. Leary, interview.

206. Woodhead, interview.

8. Reflections

207. Lamont, "Why Did the Newspaper Do That?"

208. Ibid.

209. Ibid.

210. Ibid.

211. Ibid.

212. Brice-O'Hara, testimony to Congress, September 30, 2009.

213. Ibid.

214. Ibid.

215. Ibid.

216. Ibid.

217. Gaines, "Officers Asleep."

218. USCG and Maritime Transportation Subcommittee briefing notes, September 30, 2009.

219. Brice-O'Hara, testimony to Congress, September 30, 2009.

220. Ibid.

221. "Coast Guard Training Commitment Assures the F/V Patriot's Legacy," *Gloucester Daily Times*, October 2, 2009.

222. ADM Bob Papp, interview with the author, October 5, 2021.

223. Ibid.

224. ADM Papp, email to the author, September 25, 2021.

225. "Divers Died as Party Went on Above," *Seattle Times*, January 13, 2007.

226. ADM Papp, interview, October 5, 2021.

227. Ibid.

228. Ibid.

229. USCG, *Final Action on Administrative Investigation into the Diving Mishap and the Resulting Deaths of USCGC* Healey's *Crewmembers That Occurred on August 17, 2006* .

230. Ibid.

231. ADM Papp, interview, September 7, 2021.

232. USCG Human Resources, "Flag Voice," https://www.dcms.uscg.mil/Our-Organization/Assistant-Commandant-for-Human-Resources-CG-1/Flag-Voice/.

233. Ibid.

234. ADM Papp, "Proficiency."

235. Ibid.

236. Ibid.

237. Ibid.

238. ADM Papp, interview, September 7, 2021.

Epilogue

239. Admiral Loy, speech at the U.S. Naval Institute, April 22, 1999.
240. Smith, correspondence with the author, December 5, 2021.
241. Ibid.
242. Ciaramitaro, "Gloucester's Poet Laureate John Ronan to Recite."
243. Ibid.
244. National Park Service, nps.gov.

BIBLIOGRAPHY

Newspapers and Magazines

Boston Globe
Commercial Fisheries News
Gloucester Daily Times
Portland Press Herald
Seattle Times
Soundings magazine
U.S. Naval Institute Proceedings magazine
Wicked Local

Books

Morison, Samuel Elliot. *Maritime History of Massachusetts (1783–1860)*. Cambridge, MA: Houghton Mifflin/Riverside Press, 1921.
Webster, W. Russell, and Elizabeth B. Webster. *The* Sol e Mar *Tragedy off Martha's Vineyard*. Charleston, SC: The History Press, 2014.
Yeomans, Kate. *Dead Men Tapping: The End of the Heather Lynn II*. Camden, ME: International Marine, 2004.

Articles, Websites and Blogs

Burke, Matthew. "Living Honor Heroic Coast Guard Crew." *Cape Cod Online*, February 19, 2009. http://web.archive.org/web/20120204081115/http://www.capecodonline.com/apps/pbcs.dll/article?AID=/20090219/NEWS/902190321/-1/NEWS
Check-Six.com. "Fatal Coast Guard Aircraft Accidents." https://check-six.com/lib/Coast_Guard_Aviation_Casualties.htm.

Ciaramitaro, Joey. "Gloucester's Poet Laureate John Ronan to Recite." *Good Morning Gloucester*, February 15, 2009. https://goodmorninggloucester.com/2009/02/15/gloucesters-poet-laureate-john-ronan-to-recite/.

Ciaramitaro, Joey, and Captain Joe Marcantonio. "Fifteen Years Ago Lives Were Lost Aboard the *Starbound*." *Good Morning Gloucester*, August 5, 2016. https://goodmorninggloucester.com/2016/08/05/fifteen-years-ago-lives-were-lost-aboard-the-starbound-my-cousin-joe-marcantonio-speaks-out-about-the-events-which-took-place-that-night/.

Flannery, Jim. "Coast Guard Reconstructs Mystery Sinking." *Soundings*, January 2011.

Gaines, Richard. "Close Call for Fishing Boats, Barge Fishermen Avert Collision; They Recalled *Patriot*." *Gloucester Daily Times*, March 31, 2009.

———. "Coast Guard Steps Up Access to, Training for VMS in Patriot's Wake." *Gloucester Daily Times*, June 17, 2009.

———. "Families Push for Underwater *Patriot* Photos." *Gloucester Daily Times*, January 21, 2009.

———. "Officers Asleep as *Patriot* Was Lost." *Gloucester Daily Times*, October 1, 2009.

———. "*Patriot* Family to Sue Tug Owner." *Gloucester Daily Times*, April 13, 2009.

The Gloucester Fishermen's Wives Association. gfwa.org.

Good Morning Gloucester. goodmorninggloucester.com.

Hench, David. "Hit and Run Ship Sought." *Portland Press Herald*, August 7, 2001.

Lamont, Ray. "Why Did the Newspaper Do That?" *Gloucester Daily Times*, January 17, 2009.

Loy, Admiral James. Speech at the U.S. Naval Institute, April 22, 1999. https://silo.tips/download/admiral-james-m-loy-lessons-learned-from-morning-dew-us-naval-institute-annapoli.

Marine Traffic. "What Is the Automatic Identification System (AIS)?" https://help.marinetraffic.com/hc/en-us/articles/204581828-What-is-the-Automatic-Identification-System-AIS-.

National Cold Water Safety Center. "Cold Shock." http://www.coldwatersafety.org/nccwsRules3.html.

National Park Service. nps.gov.

Papp, Admiral Robert. "Proficiency: The Essence of Discipline." *U.S. Naval Institute Proceedings*, August 2012. https://www.usni.org/magazines/proceedings/2012/august/proficiency-essence-discipline.

Prybot, Peter. "Matt's Got a New Boat." *Gloucester Times*, May 23, 2008.

Raymond, John. "What Is Hydrostatically Released Unit in Life Raft, Its Parts and Working." *Mariners Galaxy*, August 1, 2017. https://marinersgalaxy.com/wp-content/cache/all/what-is-hydrostatic-release-unit-in//index.html.

Sample, Ian. "Why Do Submarines Get Caught in Fishing Nets?" *The Guardian*, August 11, 2005. https://www.theguardian.com/science/2005/aug/11/thisweekssciencequestions.

U.S. Coast Guard. https://www.uscg.mil.

Webster, Captain W. Russell. "Too Tired to Tell." *U.S. Naval Institute Proceedings*, December 2001.

Legal Cases

Admiralty and Maritime Law Guide. *US v. Hurd and Cornett families*. Unpublished, US Court of Appeals, 4th Circuit, April 25, 2002. http://www.admiraltylawguide.com/circt/4thhurdvus.html.

Justia US Law. US District Court for the District of Massachusetts - 255 F. Supp. 737 (D. Mass. 1966) June 30, 1966. *Petition of the UNITED STATES of America, as owner of the United States COAST GUARD VESSEL CG-95321, for exoneration from or limitation of liability*. https://law.justia.com/cases/federal/district-courts/FSupp/255/737/1818251/.

Reports

Bashaw, Greg, Captain. Report to the Coast Guard. March 2009.

Brice-O'Hara, Rear Admiral Sally. Department of Homeland Security U.S. Coast Guard Statement on Coast Guard SAR Efforts before the CG and Maritime Transportation Subcommittee, U.S. House of Representatives, September 30, 2009.

National Institute for Occupational Safety and Health (NIOSH). *U.S. Commercial Fisheries Fatalities: Regional Summary, New England, 2009*. Anchorage, AK.

Niles, Katherine, USCG. *US/USA SARSAT Training Miami Beach, Florida*. January 2009.

Sandler Fisheries Inc. letter dated November 26, 2020.

U.S. Coast Guard. Air crew CG 6004 statement to the record detailing their search and recovery on January 3, 2009, undated.

———. *Commandant Instruction 16711.14 Commercial Fishing Vessel Safety*. March 3, 1993. https://media.defense.gov/2017/Mar/16/2001717327/-1/-1/0/CI_16711_14.PDF.

———. *Final Action on Administrative Investigation into the Diving Mishap and the Resulting Deaths of USCGC* Healey's *Crewmembers That Occurred on August 17, 2006*.

———. *Final Action on Administrative Investigation of the Coast Guard Response to the Sinking of the F/V* Patriot *That Occurred on January 3, 2009*. June 11, 2009.

———. *Investigation into the Circumstances Surrounding the Sinking of the F/V* Patriot. August 24, 2010. https://www.dco.uscg.mil/Portals/9/DCO%20Documents/5p/CG-5PC/INV/docs/documents/Patriot.pdf.

———. *MISLE Incident Investigation Report;* Sea Farmer II—*Loss of Auxiliary Power Equipment on October 20, 2020*.

———. Sector Boston Case Log/Chron Sheet, January 3, 2009.

———. Statement on Coast Guard SAR Efforts before the CG and Maritime Transportation Subcommittee, U.S. House of Representatives, September 30, 2009.

———. Suspicious Activity Report. July 11, 2018.

———. USCG Activity Report; MC94018454-F/V *ITALIAN GOLD*.

———. USCG Cold Exposure Survival Models for the victims, undated.

———. USCG Commandant Instruction 3500: Risk Management; March 5, 2018. https://media.defense.gov/2018/Mar/07/2001887167/-1/-1/0/CI_3500_3A.PDF.

———. USCG District One (drm) Memorandum 16130 dated January 6, 2009: SAR CASE STUDY.

———. USCG National SAR Addendum, January 2013.

———. USCG Summary of Statement (with Boston M.E.) form, September 18, 2009.

U.S. Congress, Congressional Committee Rules. 117th Congress.

U.S. Department of Homeland Security. *United States Coast Guard Navigation Rules & Regulations Handbook.* May 2020. https://www.navcen.uscg.gov/?pageName=navRuleChanges.

Interviews

Barber, Mike. Interview with the author, April 28, 2021.

Bashaw, Greg, Captain. Interviews with the author, 2021.

Cutter, Mark, BMCM. Interview with the author, April 28, 2021.

Desmond, Dave, Captain. Interviews with the author, 2021.

Doucette, Eric. Email to the author, August 25, 2021.

Gilbert, Craig, Captain. Interviews with the author, 2021.

Leary, Mike, Interview with the author, March 8, 2021.

Naccara, George, RADM. Interviews with the author, 2021.

Orlando, Dominic. Interviews with the author, 2021.

Papp, Robert, ADM. Interviews and emails with the author, 2021.

Rodolosi, Christian. Interviews and emails with the author, 2021.

Ronan, John. Interview with the author, September 2021.

Russo, Sal. Interviews and emails with the author, 2021.

Smith, Dr. Peter J. Text, email and voice correspondence with the author, 2021.

USCG Sector Boston staff. Interview with the author, March 23, 2021.

Woodhead, Jay. Interview with the author, September 10, 2021.

INDEX

A

Abromovitz, Joseph, Esq. 38, 85
acoustical analysis 11, 37
acoustical data 41
Air Station Cape Cod 31, 33, 56, 57
Air Station Operations Center 59, 60
Allen, Thad, Admiral 63
Annisquam Canal System 100
Atlantic Area Commander 53, 63, 64, 70, 80
Atlantic Ocean
    water temperatures 30, 62
Automated Mutual Vessel Reporting (AMVER) 89, 90
Automatic Identification System 37, 41, 79, 80, 95, 104

B

Barbara and Gail 65
Barker, Mike, Lieutenant 29, 33
Bartlett, Rick, rescue helicopter pilot 57
Bashaw, Greg, Captain 37, 99, 100, 101, 102, 103
Blue Force Locator 79
Boston District 29, 55, 56, 68
Boston Harbor 81, 92, 99
Boston Harbor Cruises 81
Boston Medical Examiner 33, 53
Boston Police Department 81
Brice-O'Hara, Sally, Rear Admiral 107, 108

C

Cadarina G. 61
Caffrey, District Court Judge 66
Cape Ann 19, 26, 88, 100, 107, 119
Celtic Group 42
Clark, Chris, Dr. 94
closest point of approach (CPA) 96
Coast Guard and Maritime Transportation Act of 2012 85
Coast Guard Authorization Act of 2010 85
Coast Guard Authorization Acts 109
Coast Guard City 75
Coast Guard Memorandum 55
Coast Guard Station Gloucester 10, 12, 29, 30, 31, 33, 34, 53, 55, 56, 61, 64, 70, 75, 77, 79, 84
Cold Water Exposure Models 54
commercial fishing vessel 23, 45, 82, 86, 87, 116

Commercial Fishing Vessel Safety Act of 1988 82
common operating picture 80
Communications Station (COMMSTA) 60
Cornell Bioacoustics Research program 93
Cornell University 92, 93, 94
COSPAS-SARSAT 32
COVID-19 74, 75, 115
Cummings, Elijah, Congressman 108
Cutter, Mark, BMCM 29, 33

D

Dead Men Tapping 101
Desmond, Dave, Captain 99, 100, 102
Digital Select Calling 10, 61
Doucette, Eric, Captain 75, 79, 80, 81
Doughty, Mark 90

E

Ehime Maru 41
Emergency Position-Indicating Radio Beacon 10, 28, 31, 32, 43, 44, 55, 57, 59, 60, 62, 82, 84, 89, 90, 91
Energy 11103 26, 37, 38, 96
Eulah McGrath 90

F

Federal Emergency Management Agency 10, 75
First Coast Guard District 15, 29, 53, 55, 62, 63, 106
fishing vessel/submarine interactions 36, 41, 42, 43, 129
Flannery, Jim 93
Flying Fish 29, 31, 32, 33, 60
Frontiero, Tom 90

G

Gabel, Dale, Rear Admiral 63, 71, 106, 107
Gaines, Richard 69, 103

Gilbert, Craig, Captain 62, 71, 72, 73
Global Positioning System 32, 93, 95
Gloucester, Massachusetts
   city 9, 17, 19, 20, 23, 26, 29, 30, 34, 42, 43, 45, 50, 55, 59, 75, 77, 81, 84, 96, 100, 101, 102, 107, 108, 111
   fishermen 13, 15, 19, 20, 22, 26, 43, 88, 89, 90, 99, 101, 102, 103, 105, 106, 119
Fishermen's Memorial 45, 119
Gloucester Daily Times 20, 21, 39, 63, 69, 73, 103, 104, 106, 108
Gloucester Fire Department 28, 29, 54, 55, 61
Gloucester Fishermen's Wives Association 77
Gloucester Fishing Partnership 77, 84
Gloucester Harbor 24
Poet Laureate 119. *See* Ronan, John
State Pier 19, 24, 28, 29, 91
Greenville 41
Gulf Service 26, 37, 38, 79, 92, 94, 95, 96, 99, 101, 104

H

Hammerhead 82
Healey 110, 111, 133, 137
Heather Lynn II 26, 92, 95, 101, 104
HH-3 Sikorsky 58
Houma 101
Hurd v. United States 66
Hydrostatic Release Unit 36

I

International Collision Regulations 103
International Maritime Organization 95
International Navigation Rules and Regulations 90
Italian Gold 43, 44

J

Jacqueline Robin 90
Joint Ratings Review 112

K

Kossow, Debra, Esq. 66
Kulisch, Gail, Captain 39, 53, 62, 63, 71, 74

L

Lamont, Ray 107
Leary, Mike 22, 24, 103, 104
Lee, Bill 103, 104
life raft 36, 43, 53, 61, 74, 77, 82, 89, 92
Loy, James, Admiral 116

M

Marblehead, Massachusetts 19
Marcantonio, Joseph 89, 90
Marine Autonomous Recording Units 92
Marine Casualty Investigation 37, 43, 53, 64, 74, 82, 84, 85
Marine Safety Center 42, 44
Mary & Josephine 21
Massachusetts Bay 19, 38, 93
Massachusetts Port Authority 81
Massachusetts State Police 39, 63
Merit 37, 99, 100, 101, 102, 103, 104
Middle Ground fishery 25
Miles Andrew 100
Morning Dew 12, 66, 116
M/V Sanctuary 81

N

Naccara, George, Rear Admiral 90
National Institute for Occupational Safety and Health 23
National Marine Fisheries Service 87
National Search and Rescue School 71, 115

NOAA

NOAA 28, 55, 67, 92, 95
normalcy bias 9, 10, 11, 12, 13, 14, 30, 61, 115, 116
Northern Right Whale Buoy 25

O

Ocean Reporter 103, 104
Orlando, Dominic 30, 31, 33, 34, 37, 99, 100, 101, 104
Orlando family 19, 20, 31, 33, 34, 35, 39, 42, 61, 65, 66, 73, 74, 92, 101, 119
Orlando, John 9, 13, 19, 20, 24, 25, 27, 30, 32, 34, 37, 39, 42, 43, 53, 54, 67, 84, 99, 101, 104, 119

P

Papp, Robert, Admiral 13, 53, 63, 64, 69, 70, 71, 72, 73, 74, 77, 80, 108, 109, 110, 111, 112, 113
Paschall Richardson, Isla 50
Patriot
   dockside examination 82, 84, 85
   equipment 82, 84
   last known position 9, 10, 15, 29, 57, 60, 61, 68, 69, 71, 91
   likely time of capsize 84
   machinery 85, 95
   reason for sinking 36
Prybot, Peter 20, 22

R

remotely operated vehicle 37, 39, 44
Rhiannon Rae II 39
Roberts, John, Chief Warrant Officer 75, 77
Rodolosi, Christian 19, 21, 23, 28, 34, 41
Ronan, John. *See* Gloucester, Massachusetts: Poet Laureate
Russo family 19, 20, 21, 31, 33, 35, 37, 39, 41, 42, 56, 61, 65, 66, 73, 74, 85, 92, 101, 119

Russo, Josie 9, 19, 20, 25, 26, 29, 30, 31, 33, 34, 37, 38, 41, 53, 55, 56, 61, 67, 73, 91, 92

Russo, Matteo 9, 13, 19, 20, 21, 22, 23, 24, 25, 26, 27, 29, 30, 31, 33, 34, 35, 38, 39, 42, 43, 53, 54, 61, 67, 68, 73, 84, 104, 116, 119

Russo, Sal 20, 21, 25, 26, 27, 28, 34, 41

Russo, Salvatore Moses 20

S

Salem, Massachusetts 19

Sanfilippo, Angelina 77

Sanfilippo, James 88, 89, 90

Sea Farmer II 86, 87

Search and Rescue (SAR) 53, 55, 56, 62, 64, 69, 70, 71, 72, 73, 74, 77, 78, 107, 112, 119

Sector Boston 12, 13, 29, 30, 31, 33, 39, 45, 55, 56, 57, 62, 64, 65, 73, 75, 77, 78, 81, 85, 104, 111

Sector Northern New England 86

Sennick, Marc, Commander 79

small rigid-hull inflatable boat 32

Smith, Peter, Dr. 116

Sol e Mar 11, 12, 42

Soundings magazine 93

STAAR model 58

stability 23, 36, 37, 42, 43, 44, 45, 77, 82, 85, 86, 116

Starbound 88, 89, 90, 91

Steady the Service 14, 109, 113

Stellwagen Bank National Sanctuary 11, 23, 30, 42

submarine 11, 36, 41, 42, 43, 94, 104

T

Terminator 103, 104

Theken, Sefatia 45, 75

Theriault, Paul 103

"The Salt of Gloucester" 17, 119

Time Difference on Arrival (TDOA) 94

Transportation Security Administration 10

tug 11, 26, 36, 37, 38, 41, 79, 92, 94, 95, 99, 100, 101, 102, 103, 104

Tyack, Peter, Dr. 92

U

Urgent Marine Information Broadcast 30, 56, 57

U.S. Coast Guard Navigation Rules 102, 103

U.S. Navy 11, 37, 41, 42, 44, 67

V

Vessel Monitoring System 15, 26, 29, 31, 37, 41, 54, 55, 56, 59, 60, 61, 68, 69, 72, 73, 79, 80, 88, 90, 91, 95, 101, 104, 115

Virgo 88, 89, 90

W

water temperatures. *See* Atlantic Ocean

Wayne Alarm Company 28, 29, 30, 54, 55, 67

Woodhead, Jay, Senior Controller 77, 78, 104

Woods Hole Oceanographic Institution 92

Y

Yeomans, Kate 101

Z

Zukunft, Paul, Admiral 113

ABOUT THE AUTHOR

Following a forty-five-year federal career with the Coast Guard, TSA and FEMA, Captain Webster retired in 2021, at which time he was recognized by the Department of Homeland Security with the Secretary's Outstanding Performance Award.

Captain Webster served in the Coast Guard for twenty-six years, where he was engaged in or oversaw more than ten thousand search and rescue cases and was part of a team that developed anti-terrorist doctrine. Captain Webster's articles, which have appeared in newspapers and magazines, have advocated for additional personnel for Coast Guard search and rescue teams, addressed watch stander fatigue and rescuers' post-traumatic stress and innovated small boat operational risk-based decision-making, all of which were instrumental in updating Coast Guard policies.

During his tenure at the Transportation Security Administration, Captain Webster helped inaugurate two programs that eventually evolved into nationwide initiatives: the Behavioral Detection program for passengers, and the use of TSA screeners at other transportation venues.

An International Association of Emergency Managers' lifetime-certified emergency manager, Captain Webster co-led the federal government's

COVID operations and coordinated actions of twenty-two federal agencies on behalf of six states and ten tribal nations as FEMA's Region 1 (Northeast) Administrator.

Captain Webster is a graduate of the Coast Guard Academy, where he was honored as the 2017 Distinguished Alumni. He holds master's degrees from the Naval War College and the Naval Postgraduate School.

He resides on Boston's South Shore with his family, where he continues to write and consult in homeland security and emergency management.

To learn more, visit wrussellwebster.com.